Highlights

THE HIGHLIGHTS
BIG BOOK
OF
ACTIVITIES
FOR
LITTLE KIDS

HIGHLIGHTS PRESS
Honesdale, Pennsylvania

CREDITS
Chapter Openers by Amanda Mushro ★ Art by Amanda Kay Rowe

TEXT CREDITS: Peggy Ashbrook (252–253); Lisa Danahy (138); Mairead Daugharty (111); Valerie Deneen (48–49, 279); Heather Donohue (94–95); Haeley Giambalvo (44–45); Lisa Glover (46–47, 248–249); Amanda Kingloff (24, 40–41, 52–53, 80–85, 92–93, 96–101, 240–241); Nancy Klein (144–145); Marilyn Kratz (132–133); Cara Krenn (116–117, 142–143); Heather Leann (51); Jodie Levine (90–91); Suzy Levinson (108–110); Sarah Meade (121); Amy Oldham (278); Suzie Olsen (246–247); Margaret A. Powers (254–259); Barbara L. Scanlan (136–137, 146–147); Bunny Schulle (238–239); A.B. Sisson (222); Sarah Smith (226, 244); Kimberly 73); Carol Herring (158–159); Jannie Ho (161, 184–185); Ivanke & Mey (21); Villie Karabatzia (130, 165); Brendan Kearney (114–115); Tom Knight (190–191); Gary LaCoste (108–110, 142–143); Lapin (134–135); Violet Lemay (48–49, 131, 150–151, 229); Josh Lewis (227); James Loram (152, 160, 164); Mike Lowery (25); Gareth Lucas (166–167); Berta Maluenda (26); Buff McAllister (88–89); Katie McDee (154–155); Victor Medina (12); Deborah Melmon (116–117); Mitch Mortimer (175, 188–189); Andy Passchier (105, 187); Greg Pizzoli (244); Vanessa Port (19); Alice Porter (153); Hazel Quintanilla (186); Pauline Reeves (283); Amanda Kay Rowe (12, 13, 20, 22–23, 28–30, 31, 42, 51, 52–53, 100–101, 223, 272); Erica Sirotich (132–133, 146–147, 180, 192, 271); Jacob Souva (182–183); Annabel Tempest (140–141); Ekaterina Trukhan (50, 269, 276, 284–285); Katie Turner (176–177); Marina Verola (126–127); Richard Watson (106–107, 172–173); Brian Michael Weaver (156, 168); Sam Wedelich (139, 252–253); Tim Wesson (28–29, 162–163); Karl West (113); Daniel Wiseman (14, 15, 27, 112, 128–129, 136–137, 248–249); Steven Wood (37); Olga Zakharova (193)

PHOTO CREDITS: Alamy (234, 240, 244); saguaro cactuses © Arpad Benedek 2018, All rights reserved (235); Rich Brainerd Studios (18, 34–35, 38–39, 40 –41, 44–45, 52–53, 84–85, 100–101); Jim Filipski, Guy Cali Associates, Inc. (16–17, 24, 25, 46–49, 58–59, 62–63, 66–77, 80–83, 86–95, 98–99, 254–255, 278); Getty Images (17, 24, 26–27, 37, 43, 28–29, 222–226, 228, 230–231, 234–240, 244–246, 248–249, 260–261); Alexandra Grablewski (56–57, 60–61, 64–65, 96–97, 240–241); Harmony 3 Productions (229) Andrea Killam Photography (256–259); Thomas Michael Lowery (262–263); Amanda Kay Rowe (246–247)

Published by Highlights Press
815 Church Street, Honesdale, Pennsylvania 18431
ISBN: 978-1-63962-148-4
Library of Congress Control Number: 2023945777
Manufactured in Dongguan, Guangdong, China
Mfg. 03/2024 First edition
Visit our website at Highlights.com.
10 9 8 7 6 5 4 3

Design and Art Direction: Amanda Kay Rowe
Production: Margaret Mosomillo, Gwen Moccardi, Lauren Garofano, and Tina DePew
Editors: Michelle Budzilowicz, Madison Gepper, and Andrea Silen
Managing Editor: Caitlin Conley • Copy Editor: Sarah Van Gorder
Audio Producer and Composer: Ted Weckbacher
For assistance in the preparation of this book, the editors would like to thank:
Abigail Alonso, M.A. in Curriculum & Teaching, educator; Laura J. Colker, Ed.D.,
Early Childhood Author and Consultant; and Meghan Dombrink-Green, *High Five* editor.

What Our Kids Love!

Play "Dino Breakfast" again! Again!
pages 108–110

JUNIPER
(age 2½)

I would call myself Super Teddy Chick!
page 191

ADA
(age 4)

Spy Escape: this one is my favorite because I have to do my coolest tricks.
page 37

FIONA
(age 5)

Making the magic wands was super, super, super, super fun!
pages 44–45

ATTICUS
(age 5)

Laughs and whispers
Bubbles.
shouts
Try this! Look! The BUBBLES! Did it!
page 246

FREYA
(age 2)

My boat held SO many pennies! And then it sank.
page 244

BEN
(age 3)

Which activity was *your* kid's favorite?
Send us your photos at **Highlights.com/HighFive.**

>Hey, Grown-Ups!

Your little one has boundless creativity and curiosity, and the activities in this book are designed to help harness that energy while making special moments together. Here are some tips for using this book.

Let your child take the lead.

Let your child pick activities that interest them. Read the names of the twelve chapters in the Table of Contents (pages 6–9) to your little one and ask what they'd like to do with you today.

Find the right time.

Grown-ups don't usually want to start something new when they're hungry or tired, and little kids won't either. Make sure your child is well-fed and rested before diving into a new activity.

Ask questions.

We've sprinkled open-ended questions throughout the book, but anything you ask your child can get the conversation started. Be sure to share your own thoughts as well. Your kiddo definitely wants to know what *your* favorite dinosaur is!

Have more tips to share? Join the conversation on social media with #myhighlightskid.

Embrace the mess.

We've included a "Mess Alert" on activities with paint, glitter, and other uncontrollable supplies. Don't shy away from these projects, but remember to cover your workspace first, or just plan for bath time immediately afterward!

Be kind to yourself.

Because each child has different interests and abilities, not every activity will be a winner in your home. But that's OK! Use the opportunity to learn about your child's budding personality. You're doing a great job guiding your little one through new experiences and respecting their individuality.

Celebrate process, not just progress.

There's no right or wrong way to do the activities in this book. If your child wants to add a twist to a game or do a craft with different materials, go for it! Kids learn through repetition, so be prepared to do a favorite activity over and over again.

Enjoy the little moments.

Young children are developing new skills every day. You're a huge part of helping them grow, so don't forget to embrace all the small joys that come with being their super special grown-up.

Most importantly,

Have FUN!

Table of Contents

What Our Kids Love!
3

Hey, Grown-Ups!
4-5

LET'S PLAY

Chapter Opener
10-11

The Floor Is Lava!
12

Balloon Tennis
13

Indoor Scavenger Hunt
14

Outdoor Scavenger Hunt
15

Box Bowling
16-17

Memory Match
18

Flower Power
19

Indoor Croquet
20

Human Ring Toss
21

Minute Challenges
22-23

Tic-Tac-Toe 2 Ways
24

Sponge Splash
25

Who Am I?
26

Who's That?
27

Tape Games
28-29

Boom, Clap, Grab
30

What's in the Box?
31

LET'S PRETEND

Chapter Opener
32-33

Jetpack Adventure
34-35

Fun in a Fort
36

Spy Escape
37

Stuffie Checkup
38-39

Music Maker
40-41

Construction Zone Fun
42

Excavation Station
43

Stick Wands
44-45

Grow a Garden
46-47

Superhero Costumes
48-49

Recycling Day
50

Treasure Map
51

Magic Puppet Pals
52-53

LET'S COOK

Chapter Opener
54-55

Apple Doughnuts
56-57

Animal Toasts
58-59

5 P's Pasta
60-61

Silly Snacks
62-63

Mini-Muffin Pancake Bites
64-65

Cucumber Bites
66-67

Squiggle Cookies
68-69

Banana Bites
70-71

Rainbow Pizza
72-73

Stack 'n' Snack
74-75

Veggie Bugs
76-77

LET'S CREATE

Chapter Opener
78-79

Super
Spaceship
80-81

Shaggy
Sheepdog
82-83

Recycled
Robot
84-85

Fancy
Flowers
86-87

Monster
Pals
88-89

Sky-High
Airplane
90-91

Buzzing
Bright
Bees
92-93

Mail
Truck
94-95

Make 'n' Shake
Noisemakers
96-97

Happy Birthday
Cake!
98-99

Plate-o-saurus
100-101

LET'S SING

Chapter Opener
102-103

The Itsy-Bitsy
Spider
104-105

The Rainbow
Slide
106-107

Dino
Breakfast
108-110

Rocket Trip
Surprise
111

Made of
Shapes
112

The Glumps
113

Sail with the
Letter *S*
114-115

Trash-Truck
Parade
116-117

If You're
Happy and
You Know It
118-119

Dragon Dance
120

Bandages
121

Sing-Along Lyrics
122-123

LET'S MOVE

Chapter Opener
124-125

Hero Moves
126-127

Buzz like
a Bee
128-129

Y Is for Yes
130

Fancy Clap
131

Animal Boogie
132-133

Stuffie Dance
134-135

The Partner
Fun Frolic
136-137

Crouching
Tiger
138

Handstand
Kick
139

The Plant
Dance
140-141

Surf's Up
142-143

Flop, Hop,
and Stop
144-145

Play like
Pandas
146-147

LET'S LAUGH

Chapter Opener
148-149

City Traffic Jam
150-151

Jokes
152

On My Head
153

Let's Fly a Kite
154-155

Jokes
156

Musical Friends
157

Community Garden
158-159

Tongue Twisters
160

Picnic Favorites
161

Carnival Adventure
162-163

Jokes
164

It's Pug!
165

Construction Zone
166-167

Jokes
168

Car Time
169

LET'S PUZZLE

Chapter Opener
170-171

The Soccer Game
172-173

Ollie's Garden
174

Dino Match
175

In the Garden
176-177

On the Moon
178-179

Ticket to Adventure
180

Unicorn Match
181

Birds in Hats
182-183

Time for a Carnival
184-185

Bamboo Forest
186

Doggie Match
187

Up in the Air
188-189

Super Friends
190-191

A "Cheep" Hotel
192

Big Cat Match
193

LET'S READ

Chapter Opener
194-195

Sloth Party Guide
196-199

Tasha's Library Day
200-203

Step by Step
204-206

Ocean Unicorn
207

If I Were Nocturnal
208-211

Alphabet, Interrupted
212-213

Bedtime in the Barnyard
214-218

Here Come Stars
219

LET'S EXPLORE

Chapter Opener
220-221

Nature Pattern
222

Make Pretend
Binoculars
223

Animal Homes
224-225

Reading Clouds!
226

Track
the Moon
227

Where Does
Fruit Grow?
228

1-2-3
Fruit Salad
229

How Do
Vegetables Grow?
230-231

Meet the
Dinosaurs!
232-233

Cool Habitats
234-235

Animal Families
236-237

Spotting
Shadows
238-239

Recycled Bird
Feeder
240-241

LET'S DISCOVER

Chapter Opener
242-243

Why Do
Boats Float?
244

How Does Water
Move?
245

Science
Meets Art
246-247

Fresh Water,
Salt Water
248-249

Make a Speedy
Bobsled
250-251

Pushing Is a Force
252-253

Can You
Make It Tall?
254-255

Can You
Make It Float?
256-257

Can You
Make It Move?
258-259

Hide and Seek
260-261

Seed Balls
262-263

LET'S SHARE KINDNESS

Chapter Opener
264-265

Pass It On
266-267

My Moods
268

Be Kind to Yourself
269

I'm Friendly
270

New Friend
271

Trace and Breathe
272

Toss and Talk
273

Playing at the Park
274-275

Hello, World!
276

Protect-the-Planet
Bingo
277

Mail a Hug
278

Cards That Sparkle
279

Game Time
280-281

Random Acts
of Kindness
282

A Kinder Me
283

Talk About It
284-285

What Does Your
Little Love?
286-287

LET'S PLAY

Little kids learn through play. When they're following directions, taking turns, and winning and losing, they're learning. When they're getting their wiggles out and having fun playing simple games, they're learning. When a game makes them move their body, try something new, and challenge their mind—you guessed it—they're learning. So join in and play along!

BOX AND BALL TOSS

Place boxes of different sizes around your yard. Give each box a different point value and try to throw balls or beanbags inside.

POMPOM TOSS

Write a number in the bottom of each section in an egg carton. Take turns tossing five pompoms in and aim for the biggest numbers. The highest score wins!

1 2 3
4 5 6

STUFFIE JUMP

Place a stuffie on the floor and try to jump over without touching it. Add a new stuffie for each round.

BROOMSTICK LIMBO

Hold a broom like a limbo stick while your little one walks, bends, and crawls underneath.

LET'S PLAY

What will you use to hop over the lava?

The FLOOR Is LAVA!

Number of Players: Any!

How to Play

Get from one side of the room to the other without touching the ground!

Use pillows, blankets, furniture, and other objects

as stepping stones.

LET'S PLAY

Balloon Tennis

Number of Players: 2+

How to Play

To make rackets, tape painter's sticks or rulers to the backs of paper plates. Use an inflated balloon as the ball.

How many times can you hit the balloon back and forth without letting it touch the ground?

INDOOR
Scavenger Hunt

Number of Players: Any!

How to Play

Set a timer and go on a scavenger hunt around your home. Can you find all the items before the time runs out? You can play together to find everything, or you could compete against each other.

Look for something . . .

soft	blue
you wear	smaller than a grape
bigger than a basketball	stinky
you use every day	with stripes
you play with	you can eat
that makes noise	that lights up

LET'S PLAY

OUTDOOR
Scavenger Hunt

Number of Players: Any!

How to Play

Set a timer and go for a scavenger hunt at a park or in your own backyard. Can you find all the items before the time runs out?

Look (but don't touch) for . . .

a leaf	an animal's footprint	something brown
a bird	a flower	a super long stick
something that smells good	a bug	an acorn or berry
something green	a rock or shell	something that makes noise

Box Bowling

How to Play

Before you begin: Decorate boxes with wrapping paper, paint, markers, crayons, or stickers. Stack them in a pyramid shape and roll a large ball to try and knock them all down.

1 Stack.

Stack the boxes in a pyramid shape.

Is it easier to knock down big or small boxes? Why?

LET'S PLAY

DON'T HAVE ENOUGH BOXES?

Use empty water bottles for pins instead!

FOR YOUNGER PLAYERS

Use a larger ball and stand close to the pyramid.

2 Bowl.

Roll or toss a ball toward the boxes to try to knock them all down.

Memory Match

Number of players: 2+

How to Play

Create cards out of cardstock, and make sure there are two copies of each card. Lay them upside down. Take turns flipping two cards at a time. Will you remember where the matches are?

You Need

★ Construction paper
★ Scissors
★ Two pieces of cardstock or heavy paper
★ Glue stick

1 Cut.

Cut five to ten pairs of hearts, depending on what kind of challenge you'd like.

2 Cut.

Fold and cut each piece of cardstock into equal-size cards.

3 Glue.

Glue the hearts onto the cardstock.

4 Play.

Turn all the cards face down. Take turns finding matching hearts.

Flower Power

Number of players: 2+

How to Play

Players take turns closing their eyes and pointing to a random spot on this page. The player with the highest number of points after three rounds wins!

 = 2 points

 = 1 point

= 0 points

LET'S PLAY

Indoor Croquet

Number of players: Any!

How to Play

* Use masking tape and cardstock to make several arches along the floor.
* Use a wrapping-paper tube, a broom, or another long object to hit a ball through each of the arches.

For a challenge, try gently kicking the ball through the hoops!

LET'S PLAY

HUMAN
Ring Toss

Number of players: 2+

How to Play

One person stands with their arms raised, and the other tries to toss an inner tube or Hula-Hoop around them.

What other items could you play ring toss with?

LET'S PLAY

Minute CHALLENGES

How to Play

Set a timer for one minute. Try to complete each of these challenges before the time runs out!

Spoon Run

How to Play

★ Put cotton balls on one side of the room and an empty bucket on the other.
★ With one hand behind your back, use a spoon to carry a cotton ball to the bucket. Do as many as you can!

Stick It!

How to Play

★ Stick as many sticky notes as you can in one minute all over your body.

Rice Shaker

How to Play

★ Hide a tiny object inside of a jar of rice. Make sure the lid is on tightly, and shake the jar around. Try to find the object before the time runs out.

LET'S PLAY

Ducky Balance

How to Play

★ Place a rubber duck on your head.
★ Try to balance the duck on your head until the time runs out.

Shake It Up

How to Play

★ Tear the plastic off the opening of a square tissue box.
★ Place Ping-Pong balls or rubber toys inside.
★ When the timer starts, shake the box to make the toys fall out.

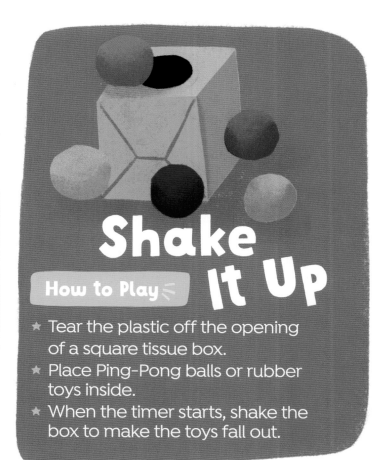

Stack 'Em All

How to Play

★ Stack as many plastic cups as you can without the tower tumbling down.

Sock 'n' Knock

How to Play

★ Set up cardboard tubes around a room.
★ Place a tennis ball in the bottom of a long sock.
★ Hold the top of the sock, and gently swing it to knock down as many tubes as possible before the time runs out.

Tic-Tac-Toe 2 Ways

How to Play

Make a tic-tac-toe board using one of the techniques below. Players take turns placing or tossing their pieces onto the board. The first player to get three of a kind in a row is the winner.

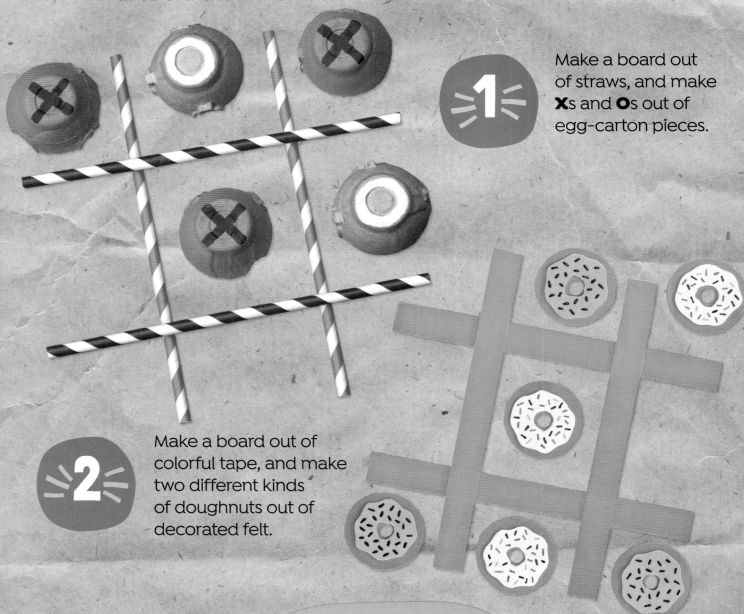

1 Make a board out of straws, and make **X**s and **O**s out of egg-carton pieces.

2 Make a board out of colorful tape, and make two different kinds of doughnuts out of decorated felt.

LET'S PLAY

Sponge SPLASH

Number of players: Any!

How to Play

★ Draw a target on the ground using sidewalk chalk.

★ After making the sponge ball, soak it in water and toss it into the center of the target.

Try to throw it with your eyes open and then with your eyes closed!

You Need

★ Sponge
★ String
★ Scissors

 **Cut.**

Cut a damp sponge into eight equal pieces.

 **Stack.**

Line up four pieces on a string. Stack four more pieces on top and tie a loose knot around the center.

 **Tighten.**

Tighten the knot, then double-knot it. Trim the excess string.

WHO Am I?

How to Play

Before you begin: Cut out or draw pictures of animals. Glue them onto an index card.

The GUESSER

★ Hold an index card on your forehead, but don't look at what's on it!

★ Use the Clue-Giver's hints to guess what's on the card you're holding up.

The CLUE-GIVER

★ Look at the card on the Guesser's forehead.

★ Give clues using actions and words. Don't say the name of the animal on the card!

* Other than animals, what things could you include on the cards?

WHO's that?

How to Play

Before you begin: Glue or draw characters onto an index card. Make three copies of each card. Place one set face-up in front of each player. Place the remaining set in the center.

The goal: Guess which animal your opponent is holding!

★ Both players should choose a card from the center set but keep their character a secret from their opponent.

★ Players take turns asking yes-or-no questions about the mystery character.

★ Use the answers to eliminate some of the cards by flipping them upside down.

LET'S PLAY

27

TAPE GAMES

Place two strips of tape on the floor.

Ask!
How far can you jump?

Don't have masking tape? Go outside and use sidewalk chalk instead!

Indoor Hopscotch

Number of players:
Any!

How to Play

★ Tape hopscotch squares on the ground.
★ Throw an object on one of the squares.
★ Hop through all the squares except the one with the object on it.

Try it with 1 foot, 2 feet, or a combination!

5

3 4

2

1

LET'S PLAY

Shape Hopper

Number of players: 2+

How to Play

★ Tape several shapes on the floor.
★ One person calls out a shape, and the other person has to jump to it.
★ Do this until you make it from one side of the room to the other.

Tangled Shapes

Number of players: 2+

How to Play

★ Cover two square tissue boxes in wrapping paper, and turn them into dice using the symbols below.
★ Add masking-tape shapes that match the shapes on Dice 2.
★ Roll the dice to find out where your hands and feet go for each round.

Dice 1 images
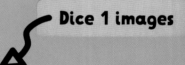

Dice 2 images

Your choice

BOOM, CLAP, GRAB

Number of players: 3

How to Play

★ Place a cup between two players. The third player calls out the words **BOOM**, **CLAP**, and **GRAB**.

★ The words **BOOM** and **CLAP** can be repeated and can be said in any order, so listen carefully!

★ The first person to **GRAB** the cup when they hear the word is the winner.

When You Hear . . .

BOOM
Hit the floor with both hands.

CLAP
Clap your hands together.

GRAB
Grab the cup in front of you before the other player beats you to it!

LET'S PLAY

What's in the BOX?

How to Play

* One person places a mysterious object in a box. (The sillier the better!)
* The other person (or people) closes their eyes while they feel inside the box. If they're prone to peeking, try a blindfold or mask.
* Can they guess what they're feeling?

How did you feel when you reached inside the box?

LET'S PRETEND

Your little one has a tremendous imagination, and you can feed their innate creativity by encouraging pretend play. When your child is pretending, they're also problem-solving, developing expressive language, and working on social and emotional development. The activities in this chapter are just a starting place, though. Your child's imagination is the only limit!

MAIL CARRIER

Create a special letter for someone. Put it in a "mail-carrier bag" and deliver it yourself.

Who will you give your letter to?

KID'S KITCHEN

Use pots, pans, whisks, and other items in your kitchen to make an imaginary feast.

What kind of meal will you whip up?

CARDBOARD BOX TRIP

Decorate a large box to look like a rocket, train, car, or something else you can travel in.

Where will you go on your pretend trip?

CIRCLE TIME

Arrange stuffed animals or dolls in a circle and pretend to be their teacher.

What will you teach your toys about?

LET'S PRETEND

Jetpack Adventure

Where will your jetpack take you?

LET'S PRETEND

* 2 two-liter bottles
* Duct tape
* Washi tape
* Tissue paper
* Double-sided tape
* Ribbon

Optional: *Before decorating, pour glitter into a wet bottle. Close the cap and shake until the sides are covered.*

MESS ALERT

1 Decorate.

Decorate 2 two-liter bottles with duct tape and washi tape.

2 Connect.

Connect the two bottles with duct tape or double-sided tape.

3 Stick.

Stick strips of tissue-paper flames to the bottle caps with double-sided tape.

TIP! Try on the jetpack and adjust the length of the straps as needed.

4 Make.

Make straps out of ribbon and duct tape.

FUN in a Fort

Use blankets, furniture, and other items in your home to create a cozy fort. Go inside and read your favorite books with a flashlight!

Spy Escape

Use painter's tape to set up yarn "laser beams" around a room. Then tiptoe, crawl, and roll your way out of the obstacle course.

For an even trickier mission, turn off the lights and use a flashlight to find your way out.

LET'S PRETEND

Stuffie Checkup

Paging Dr. Kid! Give your stuffed animals a checkup. Make bandages for their boo-boos.

Brush their teeth with a dry toothbrush and take their temperature at the checkup!

LET'S PRETEND

You Need

★ Scissors
★ Colorful felt, including white
★ Tacky glue
★ Sticky-back Velcro
★ Puffy paint

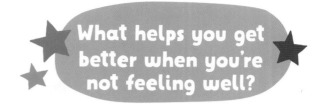

What helps you get better when you're not feeling well?

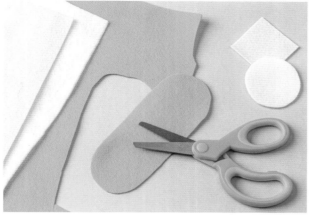

 **Cut.**

Cut bandages, white squares, and fun shapes from felt.

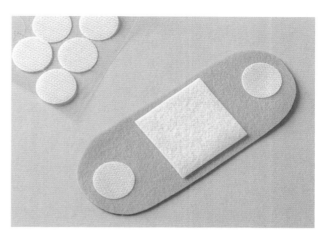

 **Glue.**

Glue a white square to the back of each bandage and glue fun shapes to the front.

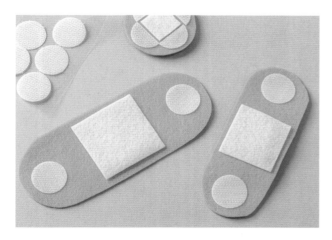

3 Stick.

Stick the scratchy part of the Velcro to the back of each bandage.

 **Decorate.**

Decorate with puffy paint. Let dry. Then stick the bandages on a fuzzy stuffie!

MUSIC
Maker

Put on a concert using items in your house. Sing into cardboard tubes, bang on pots and pans, or make a rubber-band guitar.

LET'S PRETEND

* Yogurt container
* Colored tape
* Stickers
* 3 rubber bands

1 Clean.

Clean a small yogurt container, and remove the wrapper.

2 Cover.

Cover the container with tape and stickers.

3 Add.

Add three rubber bands around the container. Then make music!

Who will you play for?

Construction Zone FUN

★ Fill a long bin with dirt, rocks, pebbles, and other objects to turn it into a construction zone.

★ Use toy construction equipment to clear paths, dig holes, lift rocks, build piles, and more.

LET'S PRETEND

Excavation Station

Bury toys in a container filled with sand. Use shovels and paintbrushes to push away the sand and search for what's inside.

Skip the sand and freeze waterproof toys in a disposable container filled with water. What are some ways you could get the toys out?

Stick Wands

Turn a stick into a wand. Decorate it using duct tape and glue as needed. Then give it a wave and let your imagination soar!

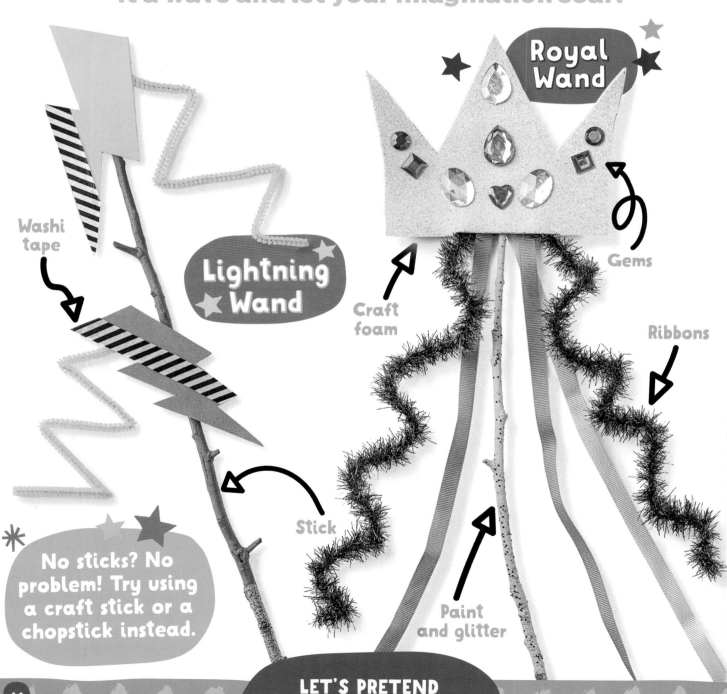

Washi tape

Lightning Wand

No sticks? No problem! Try using a craft stick or a chopstick instead.

Royal Wand

Gems

Craft foam

Ribbons

Stick

Paint and glitter

LET'S PRETEND

What kind of magical powers does your wand have?

Glow Wand

Glow-in-the-dark puffy paint

Star stickers

Weather Wand

Cardstock

Pompoms

Nature Wand

Fabric flower

Artificial vines

Fuzzy stick

Stickers

Grow a Garden

VEGGIE TIME!
Put your veggie in the cup. Pull it out to watch it "grow"!

What would you like to grow in a garden?

LET'S PRETEND

* Brown felt
* Scissors
* Craft foam

* Glue
* Paper cups
* Rubber band

Before You Begin
Grown-up: Cut a 5-inch square out of felt. Cut a + shape in the center.

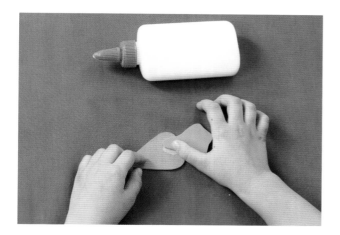

1 Cut.

Cut a veggie and a leaf from craft foam. Glue them together.

2 Snip.

Snip down the side of a cup. Then cut off the bottom.

3 Secure.

Put felt over the top of the cup and secure with a rubber band.

4 Place.

Place the cup inside another cup.

Superhero Costumes

Turn into a superhero with your own mask, cuffs, and cape.

What symbol would you wear on a superhero cape?

LET'S PRETEND

★ Craft foam or felt
★ Scissors
★ Sticky-back Velcro
★ Colored masking tape
★ Stickers
★ Towel or blanket
★ Safety pins
★ Ribbons

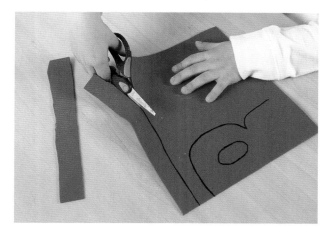

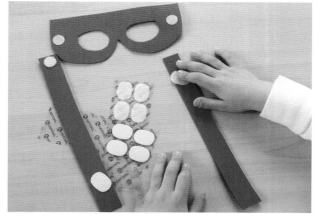

1 Cut.

Cut a mask-shape and two thin rectangle straps out of craft foam or felt for the mask. Then cut two wide rectangles for the cuffs.

2 Connect.

Using sticky-back Velcro, connect the straps to the mask and connect the ends of the cuffs together.

3 Decorate.

Use colored masking tape, stickers, and other supplies to decorate.

4 Pin.

Grown-up: Use safety pins to attach ribbons to a towel or blanket. Tie the ribbons together when wearing the cape.

LET'S PRETEND

Recycling DAY

* Scatter clean recyclables around your home or yard.
* Go on a scavenger hunt to find them.
* Pick them up with tongs or a toy grabber and sort them into different boxes.

TIP! You can sort by color, size, or material!

LET'S PRETEND

Treasure Map

What would a bird flying above your hiding spot see? Draw it on your map!

1 Hide.

Hide a special object somewhere in your yard or house.

2 Draw.

Draw a treasure map on a flattened paper bag where **x** marks the hiding spot!

3 Search.

Have a friend search for the hidden treasure.

Magic Puppet Pals

What adventures will your puppet have?

LET'S PRETEND

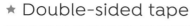

You Need

- ★ Cardstock
- ★ Cardboard tube
- ★ Double-sided tape
- ★ Scissors
- ★ Markers
- ★ Tacky glue
- ★ Sticker eyes, gems, or tissue paper

Wrap a piece of cardstock around a cardboard tube. Secure with tape.

Cut a head, snout, belly, ears, horns, and wings from cardstock. Add marker details.

Glue the snout, ears, and horns to the head. Then glue the head, belly, and wings to the cardboard tube.

Add sticker eyes, gems, or tissue-paper flames for decoration. Use tacky glue as needed.

LET'S COOK

When you cook with your child, you're teaching them important skills like following directions, counting, and measuring. Trying new recipes can also be a great way to encourage your child to try new foods. Not only can they help whip up a healthy and delicious treat that the whole family can enjoy, but they can take pride in their work.

FRUIT AND VEGGIE ART

Use fruits and vegetables to make a face or a colorful scene.

YOGURT DROPS

Line a tray with parchment paper. Add tiny drops of yogurt to the paper and freeze.

WATERMELON PIZZA

Dab the juice off of watermelon slices. Top with Greek yogurt and pieces of fruit.

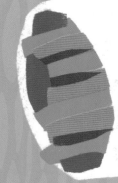

SANDWICH ROLL-UP

Use a rolling pin to flatten a piece of bread. Top with spreadable cheese and veggie slices. Then roll up the sandwich.

LET'S COOK

Naturally red foods can help your heart stay healthy.

APPLE DOUGHNUTS

LET'S COOK

* Apples
* Yogurt or nut butter
* Toppings

Before You Begin

Grown-up: Slice an apple into circles.

1 Scoop.

Use a spoon or melon baller to scoop out the center of the apple slices.

2 Pat.

Pat the slices with a paper towel to dry up extra juice.

3 Spread.

Spread yogurt or nut butter on top of the slices.

4 Add.

Add fruit, granola, coconut flakes, or any of your favorite toppings.

ANIMAL TOASTS

Use a base of toast and spreadable cheese. Add veggies to create your favorite animal.

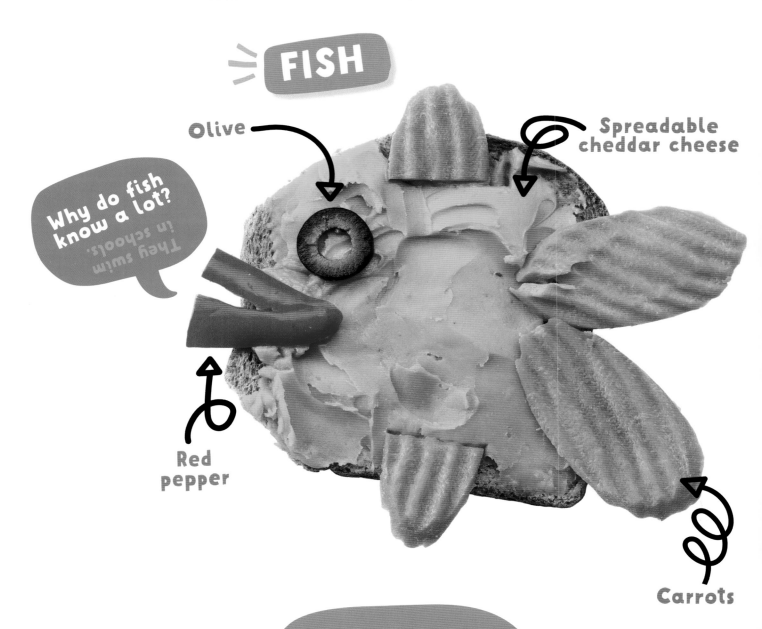

FISH

Olive

Spreadable cheddar cheese

Why do fish know a lot? They swim in schools.

Red pepper

Carrots

LET'S COOK

5 P'S PASTA

What other foods start with the letter P?

Green food can help keep bones and teeth strong.

LET'S COOK

You Need

★ Pasta
★ Peas
★ Pesto
★ Parmesan cheese
★ Pepper

Before You Begin
Grown-up: Cook your child's favorite pasta.

 **1 Scoop.**

Add two scoops of peas to your bowl of pasta.

2 Spoon.

Add a spoonful of pesto to the pasta.

 **3 Mix.**

Stir the peas, pesto, and pasta 10 times.

 **4 Sprinkle.**

Sprinkle Parmesan cheese on top. Add pepper to taste. Enjoy!

SILLY SNACKS

Spread nut butter on rice cakes and add toppings.

Pretzels

Proteins like nut butter help your muscles and bones grow.

Cereal

Blueberries

Dried apricots

LET'S COOK

Strawberries

Grape halves

Sprinkles

What's your favorite topping?

Raspberries

Mango

Coconut flakes

Bananas

Chocolate chips

LET'S COOK

Mini-Muffin Pancake BITES

Who will you share your pancake bites with?

Blue and purple foods can help your memory.

LET'S COOK

You Need

★ Pancake mix
★ Berries
★ Syrup

Before You Begin
Grown-up: Preheat oven to 350°F

MESS ALERT

1 Mix.

Make your favorite pancake mix.

2 Add.

Add the berries. Fold them into the batter.

3 Spoon.

Spoon the batter into a mini-muffin tin.

4 Bake.

Grown-up: Bake 12–15 minutes or until golden brown. Let cool. Dip your pancake bites into syrup.

Cucumber Bites

A slice of cucumber with a dollop of cream cheese makes a great snack.

Peas

Sprinkles

Cranberries

Raspberries

Cream cheese

LET'S COOK

Yummy!

Turkey

Pretzel

Olives

Pickle

Pepperoni

What will you put on top?

Squiggle Cookies

What's your squiggle cookie's name?

LET'S COOK

★ Graham crackers
★ *Optional: frosting*
★ Icing
★ Candy eyes

 Tasty!

MESS ALERT

 **1 Break.**

Break graham cracker into rectangles.

 **2 Add.**

Add frosting (optional).

 **3 Squeeze.**

Squeeze icing to make squiggles.

 **4 Place.**

Place candy eyes on icing.

Banana BITES

Cool
Cucumber and mint

Bananas help your immune system!

PB & J
Peanut butter and jelly

Rad Red
Cherries and chocolate

Yummy!

Banana Pie
Banana pudding and vanilla wafer

LET'S COOK

S'more

Graham cracker,
chocolate, and
marshmallow

**Orange
Crush**

Orange piece
and coconut
flakes

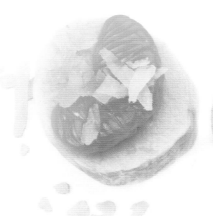

What will you
put on your
banana bites?

**The
C-C-C**

Cream cheese
and cranberries

**Kiwi
Crush**

Yogurt, kiwi,
and granola

RAINBOW PIZZA

What's your favorite color in the rainbow?

LET'S COOK

You Need

* Vegetables
* Pizza sauce
* Pizza crust
* Mozzarella cheese

MESS ALERT

1 Prep.

Set out your favorite colorful veggies.

2 Spread.

Spread the sauce on the pizza crust.

3 Sprinkle.

Sprinkle cheese evenly over the sauce.

4 Add.

Add the vegetables to make your own rainbow.
Adult: Bake for 8–10 minutes.

Stack 'n' Snack

Stack your favorite foods on a kebab stick.

Build-a-Breakfast

Whipped topping

Banana chunks

Strawberry slices

Mini pancakes

Will you create a pattern on your kebab?

LET'S COOK

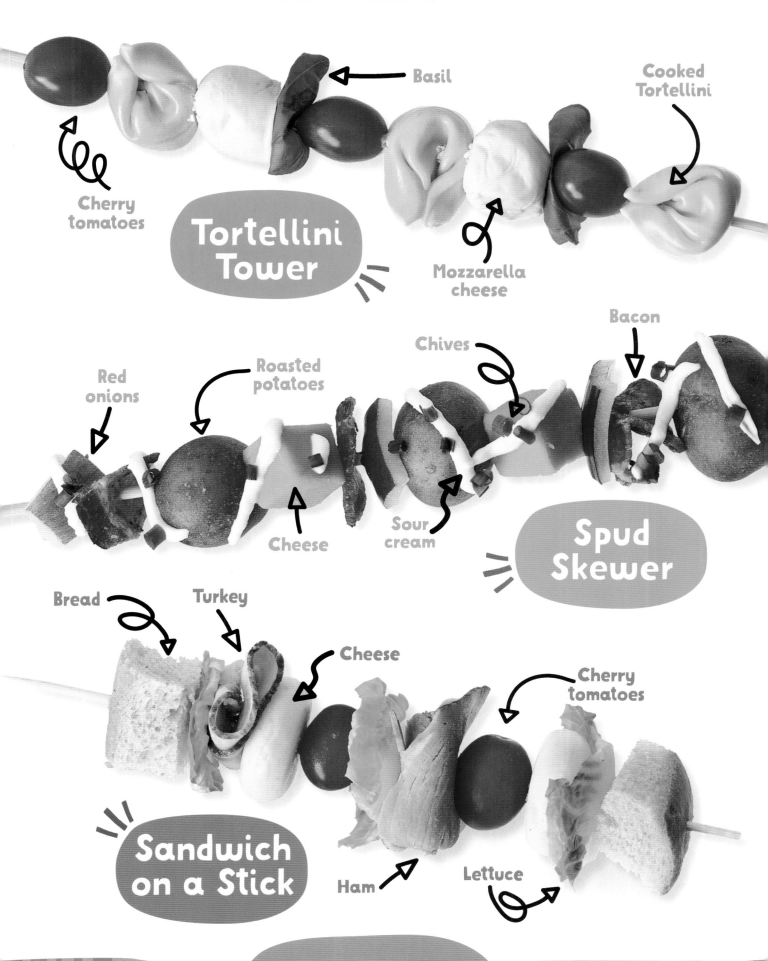

Basil

Cooked Tortellini

Cherry tomatoes

Tortellini Tower

Mozzarella cheese

Bacon

Chives

Red onions

Roasted potatoes

Cheese

Sour cream

Spud Skewer

Bread

Turkey

Cheese

Cherry tomatoes

Sandwich on a Stick

Ham

Lettuce

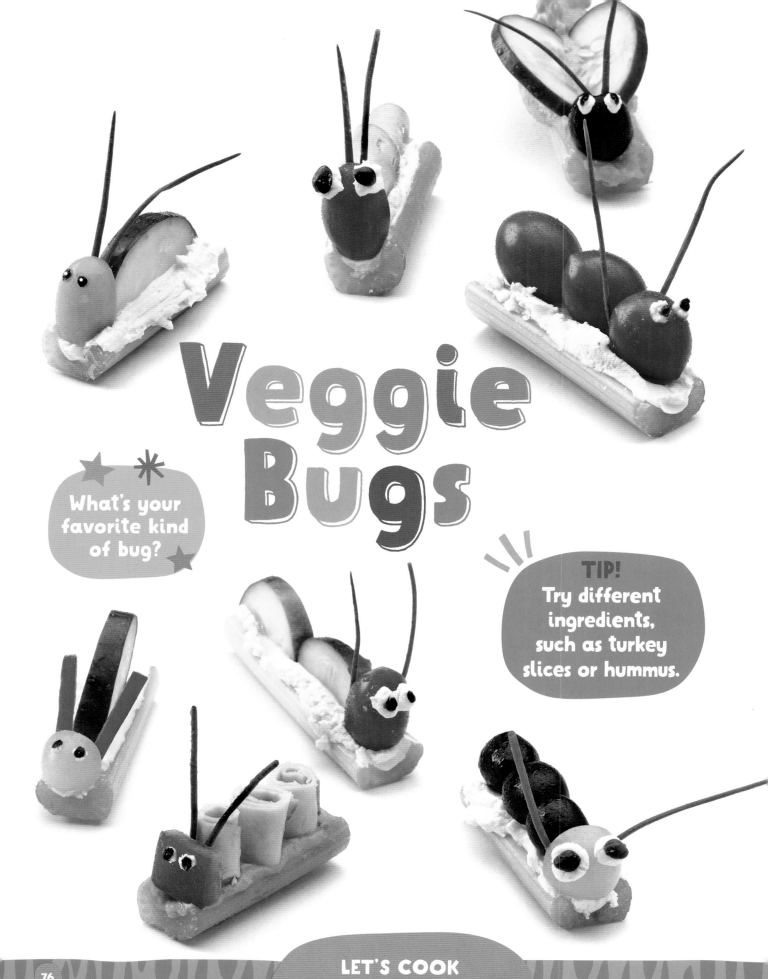

Veggie Bugs

TIP!
Try different ingredients, such as turkey slices or hummus.

LET'S COOK

You Need

* ★ Vegetables
* ★ Olives
* ★ Chives
* ★ Cream cheese

1 Cut.

Cut cucumbers into half-circles. Slice tomatoes in half. Cut celery into two-inch logs. Chop olives into small squares. Trim chives into one-inch stalks.

2 Spread.

Spread cream cheese onto celery with a butter knife.

3 Assemble.

Place cucumber and tomato on a celery log. Place chives behind the tomato (for antennae). Add cream cheese to help steady the antennae.

4 Add.

Dab cream cheese on the tomato for eyes. Then put olive squares onto the cream cheese.

LET'S CREATE

When kids paint, cut, and color, they're developing their fine-motor skills, learning to follow directions, and improving their focus and concentration. These crafts are easy to make and only require simple supplies. Be sure to praise and share what your child creates so they see their hard work on display.

FABULOUS FACES

Cut shapes from craft foam and glue them together to make faces.

POMPOM ICE POPS

Cut an ice-pop shape from cardstock. Tape a craft stick to the back. Cover the ice pop with double-sided tape and pompoms.

MESS ALERT

BOX AND BALL PAINTING

Place a piece of paper in a box with a few drops of paint and some balls on top. Tilt the box to make the balls roll through the paint.

MESS ALERT

LEAF ANIMALS

Collect leaves and paint them to look like animals.

SUPER SPACESHIP

What's one thing you'd bring on a trip to outer space?

LET'S CREATE

You Need

* ★ Cardboard tube
* ★ Colored paper
* ★ Marker
* ★ Scissors
* ★ Tape
* ★ Tissue paper

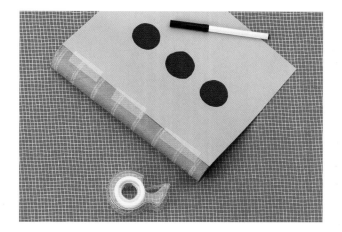

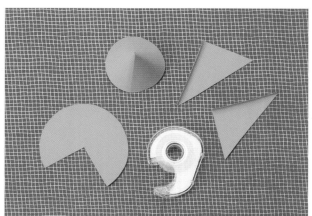

1 Decorate.

Decorate a cardboard tube. We used paper and a marker. You might use stickers or paint.

2 Cut.

Cut two right triangles for the wings. Cut a partial circle.

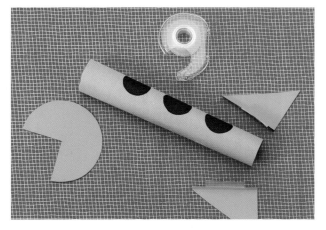

3 Tape.

Fold one side of each triangle. Tape them to the bottom of the tube. Wrap the partial circle into a cone and tape it to the top.

4 Snip.

Layer tissue paper. Pinch it near the top and tape it. Snip the ends, then crumple. Tape it inside the tube.

LET'S CREATE

SHAGGY SHEEPDOG

WOOF!

What will you name your dog?

- ★ 9 basket coffee filters
- ★ Scissors
- ★ Tape
- ★ Paper plate
- ★ Hole punch
- ★ Glue
- ★ Construction paper

1 Cut.

Fringe each coffee filter by cutting on the folds.

2 Tape.

Bunch each filter into a flower shape. Secure the bottom of each filter end with tape. Tape the filters to the plate with the fringe ends sticking out.

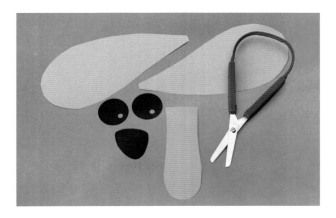

3 Cut.

Cut a pink paper tongue and gray paper ears. Cut a nose and eyes out of black paper. Use a hole punch on the eyes.

4 Glue.

Glue the eyes, nose, ears, and tongue into place. *Woof!*

RECYCLED ROBOT

Tell a story about how your robot works!

BEEP!

★ Boxes of various sizes
★ Colorful tape

★ Recyclable materials
★ Aluminum foil

★ Markers
★ Tape or glue

Before You Begin
Try drawing a blueprint or plan for the 3D robot.

1 Pick.

Pick out the boxes and recyclable materials you want for your robot.

2 Sort.

Decide which items will be the head, body, and legs.

3 Decorate.

Decorate the head, body, and legs. Try colorful tape, aluminum foil, or markers.

4 Connect.

Tape or glue the head, body, and legs together. Add arms, a hat, shoes, or anything else you want!

LET'S CREATE

FANCY FLOWERS

Who could you share these flowers with?

LET'S CREATE

Dab glue onto the center
of the cupcake liner.

Layer the mini liner onto
the cupcake liner.

Glue a pompom in the center
of the liners.

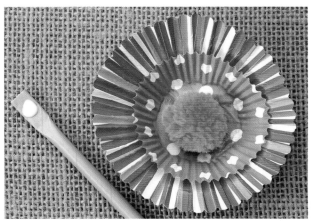

Flatten the top of the straw.
Add glue. Put the flower on top.

Monster Pals

Try out your best monster voice! What does it sound like?

LET'S CREATE

You Need

- ★ Cardboard tubes
- ★ Paint
- ★ Paintbrush
- ★ Construction paper
- ★ Pencil
- ★ Scissors
- ★ Glue
- ★ Wiggle eyes
- ★ Fuzzy sticks

Before You Begin
Grown-up: Cut a long cardboard tube into sections. Punch a hole on each side of the tube.

MESS ALERT

1 Paint.

Paint the cardboard tubes and let them dry.

2 Cut.

While the paint is drying, draw and cut out mouth and hair shapes from construction paper.

3 Glue.

Glue the mouth, hair, and eyes onto the tube. Let them dry. Glue on the teeth.

4 Push.

Push the fuzzy sticks through the holes on the sides of the cardboard tube.

LET'S CREATE

SKY-HIGH AIRPLANE

If you could fly anywhere in the world, where would you go?

LET'S CREATE

★ You Need ★

- ★ Water bottle
- ★ Construction paper
- ★ Tape or glue
- ★ Scissors
- ★ Craft foam
- ★ Circle stickers
- ★ *Optional: bottle caps and straws*

Whoosh!

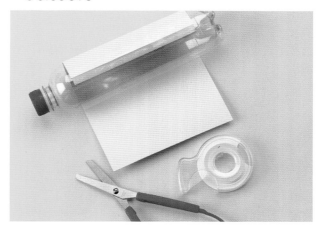

1 Cover.

Cover the bottle in construction paper. Secure it with tape.

2 Tape.

Cut wings and a tail from paper: two long ovals and one small triangle. Tape to the sides and back of the bottle.

3 Cut.

Cut a propeller shape out of foam. Cut out the inside of the circle to fit around the bottle neck. Screw the cap back on.

4 Decorate.

Add stickers for the windows. *Optional: Use bottle caps and straws to make wheels.*

What other bugs could you make?

Buzzing Bright BEES

LET'S CREATE

You Need

- ★ Egg carton
- ★ Glue
- ★ Paint
- ★ Paintbrush
- ★ Pencil
- ★ Twist tie
- ★ Bubble wrapping

Before You Begin

Grown-up: Cut out each cup from the egg carton. Glue two cups together.

MESS ALERT

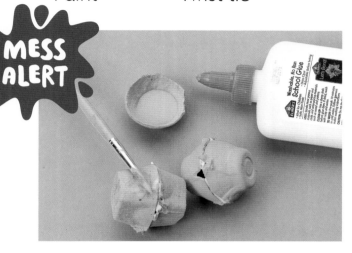

 **Paint.**

Paint the bee's body yellow. Let dry.

 **Paint.**

Paint stripes on the body. Paint eyes and a mouth. Let dry.

 **Poke.**

Use a pencil to poke a hole above the bee's face. Bend a twist tie into a V. Stick the pointed end of the V into the hole.

 **Cut.**

Cut four teardrop shapes from bubble wrapping. Glue two on each side of the bee.

LET'S CREATE

How can you show your mail carrier that you appreciate them?

Try food pouch lids and pencils to make wheels that roll!

LET'S CREATE

- ★ Cereal box
- ★ White paper
- ★ Glue stick
- ★ Scissors
- ★ Double-sided tape
- ★ Blue construction paper
- ★ Markers
- ★ Colorful tape
- ★ 4 recycled caps

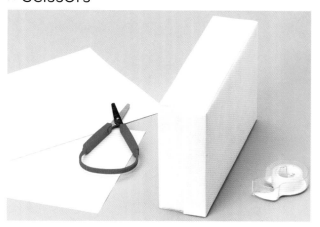

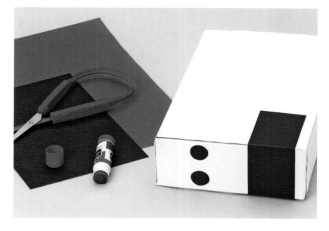

 **Cover.**

Cover the cereal box with white paper. Secure with tape or glue.

 **Cut.**

Cut a long rectangle (windshield) and two small circles (headlights) from blue construction paper. Glue them onto the truck.

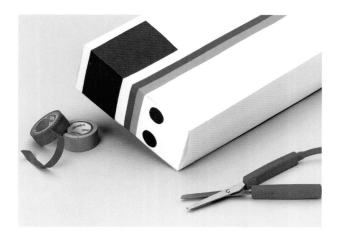

 **Add.**

Add stripes with markers or colorful tape.

 **Attach.**

Attach the caps (wheels) to the box with double-sided tape.

Make 'n' Shake
Noisemakers

What other noisy objects could go inside?

LET'S CREATE

You Need

★ Small jewelry box
★ Buttons, dried beans, or rice
★ Tape
★ Craft stick
★ Stickers

Hooray!

1 Place.

Place buttons, dried beans, or rice into a small box.

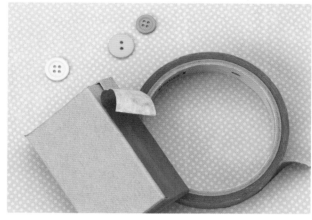

2 Tape.

Tape the box tightly.

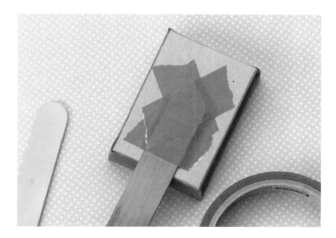

3 Tape.

Tape a craft stick to the back of the box.

4 Decorate.

Decorate the box with stickers. Then shake it!

Happy Birthday CAKE!

What else could you do at a pretend birthday party?

LET'S CREATE

You Need

* Cardboard tube
* Colorful tape
* Scissors
* Construction paper
* Pencil ★ Glue
* Paintbrush
* Fuzzy sticks
* 2-inch paper straw section
* Pompom

Before You Begin

Grown-up: Cut a cardboard tube into two-inch sections. Then cover each section in tape.

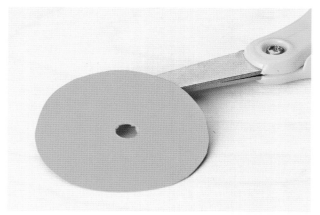

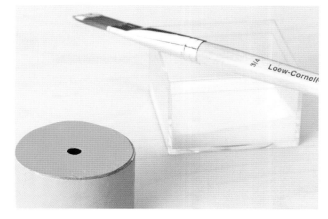

1 Trace and Cut.

Stand a taped tube section on construction paper. Trace the bottom, cut out the circle, and punch a hole in it.

2 Trace and Glue.

Brush glue on the circle. Glue the circle to the top of the tube.

3 Wrap.

Wrap a fuzzy stick around the top of the tube. Twist and trim the excess. Repeat at the bottom.

4 Decorate.

Create a candle by gluing a pompom to the top of a straw. Insert the straw in the hole. Then decorate your cake!

plate-o-saurus

What's your favorite kind of dinosaur?

LET'S CREATE

>You Need<

- ★ Paper plates
- ★ Scissors
- ★ Cardstock
- ★ Tape
- ★ Markers
- ★ Glue

Tip!
Use a hole punch to make dots.

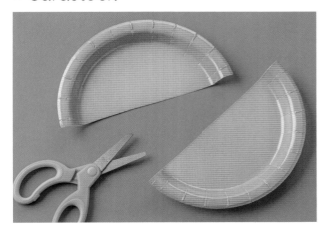

 **1 Cut.**

Cut a dinosaur body out of a paper plate.

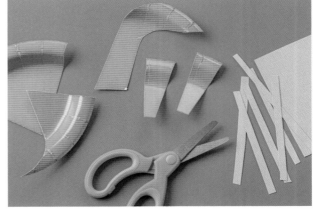

 **2 Make.**

Make legs and a head from paper-plate pieces. Then cut other decorations from cardstock.

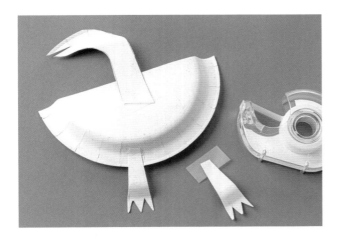

 **3 Tape.**

Tape the legs and head to the paper-plate body.

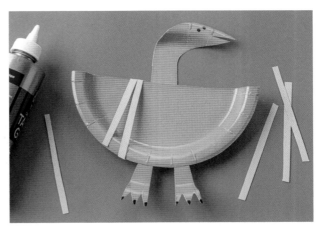

 **4 Add.**

Add marker and cardstock details for decoration. Use glue as needed.

LET'S SING

Even if you can't carry a tune, your little one loves to sing with you. Singing helps kids learn new words and stretches their memory and focus. All of these skills are super important because they help lay the foundation for learning to read. Plus, you can take these songs wherever you go!

Scan to hear all the songs in this chapter.

TAKE A SOUND WALK

The next time you go for a walk, close your eyes and listen carefully. Talk about the sounds you hear, and see if you can recreate the sounds with your own voices!

GO ON A RHYTHM HUNT

Look around your home for everyday objects that you can drum, shake, tap, scrape, or jingle.

TRY dried beans in a clean water bottle or wooden spoons on pots and pans!

LISTEN TO THE BEAT

Paint cardboard boxes of various sizes with poster paint. Decorate your drums with markers or stickers. Use wooden spoons or paint stirrers as drumsticks to make your own music!

Do boxes of different sizes sound the same or different?

CLEANUP WITH A TWIST

Turn cleanup time into a game by playing a freeze-dance song. When the music stops, freeze until the music starts again. Race to clean up as much as you can before the music stops!

LET'S SING

The Itsy-Bitsy Spider

The itsy-bitsy spider went up the waterspout.

Down came the rain . . .

. . . and washed the spider out.

Out came the sun, and dried up all the rain.

And the itsy-bitsy spider went up the spout again.

LET'S SING

Make up your own actions for these bugs!

The itsy-bitsy inchworm
climbed up the flower stem.

Whoosh came the wind
and blew her down again.

Out came the sun.
The wind came to a stop.

And the itsy-bitsy
inchworm climbed
right back to the top.

The teensy-weensy cricket
chirped the whole night long,

rubbing his wings
to play his favorite song.

Up rose the sun.
It's time for cricket's bed.

So the nocturnal bug
went off to rest his head.

The twinkly-twinkly firefly
glowed as nighttime fell,

casting warm light—
a magic sparkling spell.

Out came the moon
and added to the light,

while the twinkly-twinkly
firefly shone throughout the
night.

The busy honeybees flew
all around the air.

Landed on a flower,
collected nectar there.

Flew to their hive
to feed the other bees.

And then they made
some honey, the perfect
sticky treat.

LET'S SING

The RAINBOW Slide

Let's jump for **RED, ORANGE, YELLOW,** and **GREEN.**

BLUE, PURPLE, PINK, BROWN, stomp your feet.

LET'S SING

Think of a food for every color of the rainbow.

BLACK and **WHITE**, side to side.

Everybody move to The **RAINBOW** Slide.

LET'S SING

107

Dino Breakfast

Crunch

Munch

MILK

Cereal-saurus wanders the plains, grazing for cornflakes and great-tasting grains. Crunchy-o trees and a whole-milk stream.

LET'S SING

Fruity-o-saurus lets out a roar,
chomping on apples, bananas, and more.
Tropical fruits, with herbivore roots.

Whoosh

Come on down to the
Diner Jurassic. The Eggs
Stegosaurus is a fossil
sauce classic. *Triceratops*
Toast is what you'll
crave the most.

LET'S SING

Cinnamon-saurus glides coast-to-coast, hunting up buttery cinnamon toast.

Dinosaurs start out their day with a munch, stomping and chomping away with a crunch. First comes some breakfast . . . next, some dino lunch.

Come on down to the Diner Jurassic. The Eggs *Stegosaurus* is a fossil sauce classic. *Triceratops* Toast is what you'll crave the most.

LET'S SING

ROCKET TRIP SURPRISE

To the tune of "Yankee Doodle"

I took a trip
to outer space,
riding on
a rocket.
I looked for
other planets,
and I flew right by
a comet.

I rode my rocket
to the moon,
flying fast
and far.
I passed some
asteroids on
my way,
and counted
all the stars!

I geared back
up to leave the
moon,

and hopped back
in my rocket.
Set course for
the next planet,
and blasted
into orbit.

Goodbye,
moon, we've
had some fun!
I'm headed
straight for Mars.
I checked my
pocket on
the way—
surprise! I
found a star!

MADE of SHAPES

Move that robot head side to side.

Robots, stop, and bend your knees.

Put your robot arms out straight. Bend them up halfway.

Now, robots, move around and around . . . and freeze!

LET'S SING

THE GLUMPS

We are the Glumps,
we are the Glumps,

and we're here to
help you clean up
this dump.

Have no fear 'cause
the Glumps are here,

and together we'll
make this mess
disappear!

LET'S SING

Sail with the Letter S

LET'S SING

So sing with me this song of the sea,
and we'll put our skills to the test.
And heave-ho to the stars we'll go,
as we sail with the letter *S*.

What things in groups of 7 do you see?

LET'S SING

Trash-Truck
PARADE

Come on, everybody, today's the day.
Let's head outside for the Trash-Truck Parade!
Rumble, rumble down the street,
here come the trucks for us to meet.

LET'S SING

Recycling Truck

Compost Truck

Trash Truck

What trucks do you see where you live?

If You're HAPPY and You Know It

If you're happy and you know it . . .

Clap your hands.

Stomp your feet.

Nod your head.

Do all three!

LET'S SING

If you're sad
and you know it,
hug a friend.

If you're friendly
and you know it,
share a toy.

If you're grumpy
and you know it,
take a breath.

If you're playful
and you know it,
run around.

If you're sleepy and
you know it,
take a snooze.

LET'S SING

Dragon DANCE

What noise would a dragon make?

Dragons snooze.

ROAR!

Dragons roar.

STOMP! STOMP!

Dragons stomp like a dinosaur.

Shake! Shake!

They shake their tails.

Flap! Flap!

And they flap their wings.

Dragons do a lot of silly things.

LET'S SING

Bandages

Bandages on boo-boos,
bandages on scrapes.
Bandages with crowns,
bandages with capes!

Bandages on ouchies,
bandages on bites.
Bandages for mermaids, too,
and bandages for knights!

Bandages both big and small,
if you scrape your knee,
or trip and fall.
A boo-boo, a scrape,
a scratch, or cut,
those bandages will help
heal them up.

Bandages on hands,
bandages on feet.
Bandages for creatures,
in the air or under the sea.

Bandages on elbows,
bandages on knees.
Bandages are gone?
We need a bandage
refill, please!

LET'S SING

The Rainbow Slide

Let's jump for red, orange, yellow, and green.
Blue, purple, pink, brown, stomp your feet.
Black and white, side to side.
Everybody move to The Rainbow Slide.

Ladybug, stop sign, fire truck: Red!
Carrots, tigers, and
    pumpkins, too: Orange!
School buses, lemons, and
    the sun: Yellow!
Turtles and frogs: Green!
The ocean: Blue!

We've got grapes and
    a purple sea star:
    Purple!
Flamingos and a
    cute little pig: Pink!
What about a muddy mess?
    Brown!
The spots of a cow: Black!
The clouds in the sky: White!

The Glumps

You look outside your window,
    and the sun is shining through.
But before you play, you got chores today, and
    you have to clean your room.
What if I were to tell you that your chores can be
    fun, too?
When you're in a slump, you just call the Glumps,
    they'll make everything good as new.

And they'll sing:
"We are the Glumps, we are the Glumps,
    and we're here to help you clean up this dump.
Have no fear 'cause the Glumps are here.
And together we'll make this mess disappear!"

Here's what happened to me.
Into my room slumped seven Glumps,
    little jumpy creatures all made of lumps.
They picked up clothes from here and there.
They even folded my underwear.

I put my toys back in the bin,
    and they helped me make my bed.
They vacuumed the floor
    and cleaned the closet, too.
I couldn't believe what these
    Glumps could do!

Made of Shapes

My robot head is made of shapes,
    round circle eyes on a square face.
With triangle ears, you can't go wrong,
    and a rectangle mouth, two sides short,
    two sides long.

Move that robot head side to side.
Now, robots, stop, and bend
    your knees.
Put your robot arms out straight.
    Bend them up halfway.
Now, robots, move around and
    around … and freeze!

My robot body is made of shapes,
    a square belly, each side the same.
Oval buttons and circle gears,
    long rectangle legs with triangle knees.

Now, robots, move up and down … and freeze!
And robots move around real slow …
    and freeze!
Now, robots, move down real low … and freeze!
Now, robots, groove around and around …
    and freeze!

Sail with the Letter S

Sally the savviest sailor,
    she sailed the seven seas.
She set out from Spain in the summer,
    and she didn't return 'til next spring.

So sing with me this song of the sea,
    and we'll put our skills to the test.
And heave-ho to the stars we'll go,
    as we sail with the letter S.

Now Sally went searching for treasure.
She stuck her spade in the sand.
She stopped to snack on a sandwich,
    then a snake slithered up, so she ran.

So sing with me the song of the sea,
    and we'll put our skills to the test.
And heave-ho to the stars we'll go,
    as we sail with the letter S.

Sing-Along Lyrics

Scan to hear all the songs in this chapter.

Trash-Truck Parade

Come on, everybody, today's the day.
Let's head outside for the Trash-Truck Parade!
Rumble, rumble down the street,
   here come the trucks for us to meet.

First comes recycling in a truck that's blue!
It takes used stuff to make something new.
Bottles and cans, papers and tins,
   the truck lifts it up, then dumps it all in.

Next comes the driver in a truck that's green.
He puts our old plants in the mulch machine.
Our grass and leaves and tree clippings
   become compost and mulch and new
   wood chippings.

Come on, everybody, today's the day.
Let's head outside for the Trash-Truck Parade!
Rumble, rumble down the street,
   here come the trucks for us to meet.

Last comes the truck that's big and gray.
It moves our junk to the landfill today.
All our scraps and all our trash
   go up in the truck with a great big *CRASH*!

The happy workers honk and wave.
We jump up and down and shout, "Hooray!"
"See you next week," we smile and say.
"We'll be back outside on Trash-Truck Day."

   Come on, everybody, today's the day.
Let's head outside for the Trash-Truck Parade!
Rumble, rumble down the street,
   here come the trucks for us to meet.

Let's head outside for the Trash-Truck Parade.
Let's head outside for the Trash-Truck Parade.

If You're Happy and You Know It

If you're happy and you know it,
   and you really want to show it,
if you're happy and you know it, clap your
   hands, stomp your feet,
   nod your head, and do
   all three!

If you're sad and you
   know it,
   and your face will
   surely show it,
if you're sad and you
   know it, hug a friend.

If you're friendly and you know it,
   and you really want to show it,
   if you're friendly and you know
   it, share a toy.

If you're grumpy and you know it,
   and you're trying to control it,
   if you're grumpy and you know it,
   take a breath.

If you're playful and you know it,
   and you really want to show it,
   if you're playful and you know it, run around.

If you're sleepy and you know it,
   and your eyes are slowly closin',
   if you're sleepy and you know it, take a snooze.

Dragon Dance

Dragons snooze. Dragons roar.
Dragons stomp like a dinosaur.
They shake their tails, and they
   flap their wings.
Dragons do a lot of silly things.

So dance, dance like a dragon,
   dance!
Get your tails a-waggin'!
(*Chorus 2:* Get your wings a-flappin'!)
Dance, dance like a dragon.
Everybody clap your hands and do the
   dragon dance.

Now everybody snooze. Everybody roar.
Everybody stomp like a dinosaur.
Now shake those tails, and flap your wings.
Everybody do silly dragon things.

LET'S MOVE

When little kids have trouble sitting still, it's important for them to get the wiggles out! These movement activities offer plenty of ways to help your child have lots of fun while they burn some energy. The best part of these activities is that you don't need expensive equipment or to even leave your house to get your kids moving and grooving.

BALL TOSS

Hold the edges of a small blanket or towel and toss a soft ball on top. Shake the blanket and make the ball move!

BALANCING ACT

Balance a book on your head for as long as you can. What else can you balance?

FLAMINGO STAND

Put one foot on the ground and lift the other one. Stretch out your arms for balance.

TAPE WALK

Place a long strip of tape on the floor. Walk along it like a balance beam.

LET'S MOVE

125

Hero

Superheroes like to stand tall.

Superheroes are brave and strong.

LET'S MOVE

Moves

What superhero power would you like to have?

And when they're all finished saving the day,

they use their powers to fly far away.

Buzz like a Bee

Fly around fast, and *buzz* like a bee.

Land on a flower. Dance happily!

How many bees can you count?

Scoop up pollen.
Hold on to it tight.

Fly back to the hive,
and say good night.

LET'S MOVE

Y Is for YES

What letters can you make with your body?

What letters can you make with a friend?

P

K

A

H

LET'S MOVE

Fancy CLAP

Lift your leg, then clap your hands under your leg.

What other fun ways can you clap?

Animal Boogie

If you love your special stuffie, hold it high.

Take it flying ziggy-zaggy through the sky!

STUFFIE

LET'S MOVE

You can twirl it nice and slow.
Now it's time to sink low.

Then give your friend a hug
and wave goodbye!

DANCE

The Partner

Face your partner.

Take a bow.

Hands on hips,

then circle round.

LET'S MOVE

Fun Frolic

Tap your elbows.

Now you twist.

Clap your hands.

Raise your wrists.

Crouching TIGER

How does this make you feel?

Hide in the tall grass.
Get your claws ready.
Make your eyes big.
Crouch down and say

GRRR!

LET'S MOVE

Handstand Kick

Can you kick your legs in the air while standing on your hands?

What other animals kick their back legs?

LET'S MOVE

The Plant Dance

Wave like a palm tree dancing in the breeze.

Float to the ground like a leaf from the trees.

LET'S MOVE

Surf's Up

Paddle, paddle out to sea.

Jump up on your feet.

Now bend your knees.

LET'S MOVE

FLOP, HOP, AND STOP

Twist and turn.

Stretch …

then flop.

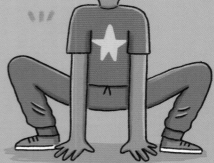

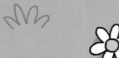

LET'S MOVE

PLAY LIKE PANDAS

Playful pandas play peekaboo.

LET'S MOVE

They eat tall shoots of sweet bamboo.

Playful pandas stomp, stomp, stomp.

Playful pandas roll and romp!

LET'S LAUGH

Laughing together is a great way to bond with your child, and when things don't go as planned, having a sense of humor can help your child cope with difficult situations. From classic jokes to activities that tickle the funny bone, you and your child will be sharing lots of giggles. There are no right or wrong answers when it comes to humor—just enjoy your child's silliness!

GOOFY GRINS

Cut out silly facial features from construction paper. Use painter's tape to stick them to things around your home. Add wiggle eyes for extra fun!

SILLY-STEPS TAG

Whoever is "It" chooses a silly walk for the first round. All the players must do the silly step—no running! Once whoever is It tags another player, that player decides what the next silly step will be.

SILLY-STEP IDEAS

TIPTOE

CRAB WALK

SKIP

HOP

DON'T LAUGH!

Stand back to back. On the count of three, turn and face each other. Make silly faces to get the other player to laugh first.

NONSENSE WORDS

Choose a silly word to replace with another word. For example, a book could be called a *readabuncha* or a bath could be called a *splishsplash*. Try to use the word as much as possible for a day!

City Traffic Jam

LET'S LAUGH

JOKES

Why did the chicken cross the playground?

To get to the other slide.

Why did the cow cross the road?

To get to the udder side.

HA HA HA

Why did the farmer cross the road?

To fetch his lost chicken.

HA HA HA

LET'S LAUGH

On My Head

Hair clip on the head

Hat on the head

Party hat on the head

Pineapple on the head?

WHOOPS!

Let's Fly a Kite

LET'S LAUGH

What silly things do you see?

JOKES

Knock, knock.
Who's there?
Interrupting cow.
Interrupting c—
MOOOOOOO!

Knock, knock.

Who's there?

Cows go.

Cows go who?

No, owls go *who.* Cows go *moo!*

HA HA HA

HA

HA HA

HA HA HA

Musical Friends

Saxophone

Xylophone

Drum

Celery?

Community Garden

LET'S LAUGH

What silly things do you see?

TONGUE TWISTERS

Say each tongue twister three times fast!

Llama mama loves little llama.

Goose's groovy green guitar jams!

Bunny bakes banana bread.

Dog dove deep.

LET'S LAUGH

Whoops!
Picnic Favorites

Watermelon

Macaroni Salad

Burgers

Mustard-Ketchup Ice Pop?

Carnival Adventure

LET'S LAUGH

What silly things do you see?

JOKES

What's black and white and black and white and black and white?

A panda rolling down a hill.

What's black and white and red all over?

A zebra with a sunburn.

HA HA HA

What's black and white and read all over?

A newspaper.

What's black and white and blue all over?

A shivering penguin.

HA HA

Whoops! It's Pug!

What words do you hear that rhyme?

Pug on a rug.

Pug with a mug.

Pug next to Doug.

WHOOPS!

Pug sits on Bug?

Construction Zone

LET'S LAUGH

LET'S LAUGH

JOKES

LET'S LAUGH

Whoops!
Car Time

Small Car

Square Car

Tall Car

Banana Car?

LET'S PUZZLE

Spotting all the objects in a Hidden Pictures puzzle or figuring out all the twists and turns in a maze helps build confidence, teach perseverance, and develop attention to detail. These visual puzzles are designed to be completed without a pencil or crayon—so your child can do the puzzles over and over again, sharpening their problem-solving skills.

STICKER PATTERNS

Make patterns using stickers. Let your child add the last sticker to complete each pattern.

CRAFT-STICK PUZZLE

Tape craft sticks together, then draw a picture on them. Remove the tape, scramble the craft sticks, and put the picture back together.

You can also draw a picture on cardboard and then cut it into pieces.

TOY MATCHING

Trace outlines of favorite toys onto a piece of paper. Take turns matching the outline with the correct toy.

TAPE MAZE

Make a maze with painter's tape on the floor. Race toy cars through the maze from start to finish.

The Soccer Game

Pizza

Kite

Ice-Cream Bar

Candle

Heart

LET'S PUZZLE

Find the objects hidden in the picture!

Banana

Snake

Pencil

Sock

What sports are played with a ball?

LET'S PUZZLE

Ollie's Garden

Oscar is meeting his friend Ollie. Can you help him find a path to Ollie's garden?

LET'S PUZZLE

Dino Match

Every dino here has one that looks just like it. Find all 5 matching pairs.

Would a dinosaur be a good pet? Why or why not?

In the Garden

LET'S PUZZLE

How are these pictures the same?
How are they different?

On the Moon

Comb

Ruler

Toothbrush

Paintbrush

Lollipop

LET'S PUZZLE

Find the objects hidden in the picture!

Envelope

Baseball

Plate

Teacup

What would you take with you on a trip to outer space?

LET'S PUZZLE

Ticket to Adventure

Tiger's Travel Agency is packed today! Follow the paths to see where each tourist is going.

CHEESE TOUR

LAZY RIVER Getaway

SWIM   FLOAT   CHILL

Flower Garden

SAFARI ADVENTURE

Unicorn Match

Every unicorn here has one that looks just like it.
Find all 5 matching pairs.

Where would you
go on a playdate
with a unicorn?

Birds in Hats

LET'S PUZZLE

LET'S PUZZLE

Time for a Carnival

Ruler

Heart

Muffin

Banana

Pizza

LET'S PUZZLE

Find the objects hidden in the picture!

Golf Club

Button

Cane

Comb

What's your favorite carnival ride?

Bamboo Forest

Perry wants to eat bamboo with his friend. Can you help him find a clear path through the bamboo forest?

FINISH

START

LET'S PUZZLE

Doggie Match

Every dog here has one that looks just like it.
Find all 5 matching pairs.

Do you think dogs enjoy music? Why?

Up in the Air

LET'S PUZZLE

How are these pictures the same? How are they different?

Super Friends

Pizza

Doughnut

Lollipop

Almond

Broccoli

LET'S PUZZLE

Find the objects hidden in the picture!

Pencil

Kite

Envelope

Snail

What would your superhero name be?

LET'S PUZZLE

191

A "Cheep" Hotel

The bus is packed with travelers ready to start their vacations. Can you help the bus find a path to the hotel?

LET'S PUZZLE

Big Cat Match

Every cat has one that looks just like it.
Find all 5 matching pairs.

In what ways are you like a cat?

LET'S READ

Reading for at least 20 minutes every day helps foster a love of reading. Your child loves hearing you read to them, and it also helps build attention skills and language and literacy skills. Whether you make silly sounds and voices or snuggle up together and read quietly, reading time is special because you're doing it together.

GO ON A LETTER HUNT

Pick a letter and look for items that start with that letter sound. Take a picture of each item and create a photo book for the whole alphabet.

SENSORY FUN

Fill a tray or baking sheet with a thin layer of salt or sand. Draw letters on an index card. Then use fingers or a paintbrush to recreate the letters in the salt or sand.

WORD OF THE DAY

Pick a new word each day and write it out on a piece of paper. Any time you see the word that day, read it aloud together.

Start with a favorite animal or a word that starts with the same letter as your child's first name.

TELL A SILLY STORY

Draw pictures or words on pieces of paper and put them in a basket. Take turns picking out a piece of paper. Use it as inspiration to tell a story. The sillier the better!

Sloth Party Guide

By Carrie Williford ★ Art by Monika Filipina

If you want a sloth to come to your party on a Wednesday, tell him to be there by Tuesday. (As we all know, sloths are usually late.) Sloths are the slowest mammals on the planet, so you have to give them plenty of time to get to a party.

LET'S READ

If you're going to throw a party for a sloth, be sure to have the snacks he likes. Put a nice, big plate of leaves on the table, and you'll have a happy sloth.

If it's hot, make it a pool party! Sloths are great swimmers.

As for inviting other party guests, the sloth would be delighted to see two of his closest relatives, the anteater and the armadillo.

LET'S READ

What are all the things you should do for a sloth party?

And last, to make a sloth feel welcome, the most important thing to have is a nice, sturdy branch. A sloth will insist on the longest branch you can find. This way, everyone can hang out with him. What a party!

LET'S READ

Tasha's Library Day

By Marisa Frederickson ★ Art by Andy Passchier

Tasha is excited—today is Library Day! Tasha knows exactly what will happen. First, she'll pick out lots of books. Tasha will sing, "I want this one and that one, this one and that one." Tasha's mom will balance their tall tower of books.

Next, Tasha will sit in her favorite yellow chair. Then, she'll read until both hands on the clock point to twelve.

LET'S READ

LET'S READ

When they arrive at the library, Tasha looks for her favorite chair.

"Someone's in my chair!" says Tasha.

"I know you like the big yellow chair, but these chairs belong to everyone," says Tasha's mom. "Let's find another chair for you to read in."

Tasha's eyes fill with tears. She looks around the room before spotting a giant red floor pillow. Tasha wipes the tears from her face and takes a deep breath.

"I'm going to try that red pillow," she says.

"Go for it!" says Mom.

LET'S READ

What happened in the beginning, middle, and end of the library day?

When both hands point to twelve on the clock, Tasha's mom comes over. "Do you like what you're reading?" she asks. "Yes, and I like where I'm reading," says Tasha. "It's my new favorite!"

LET'S READ

Step by Step

By Maggie Murphy ★ Art by Zachariah OHora

Squirrel had a new tree house. "Please come up and look inside," she said to Chipmunk, her friend and next-door neighbor.

"I wish I could," said Chipmunk. "But I can't."

"Maybe sometime tomorrow?" asked Squirrel.

"I can't at all, ever." Chipmunk stared at the ground. "It's such a long way up that I'm kind of scared."

Squirrel thought awhile. Finally she said, "Want to practice going up? We could climb a little of the way now and come right back down. Then we'd climb higher each day."

"Let's try it," said Chipmunk.

So they climbed five steps toward the tree house, and came down. When Chipmunk's feet touched the ground, the friends said, "Hooray!"

On the second day, they climbed ten steps, and came down. "Hooray!"

On the third day, they climbed fifteen steps, and came down. "Hooray!"

What new thing could you try to do step by step?

The fourth day came. They started climbing. "We're almost there," said Chipmunk, "and I'm not scared." Soon they were inside the tree house.

"Hooray! You did it!" said Squirrel.

"Thanks, Squirrel. And it's a wonderful house!"

LET'S READ

Ocean Unicorn

By Diana Murray ★ Art by Gareth Lucas

A narwhal often has a tooth that sticks out like a horn, which makes it look a little like an ocean unicorn.

It swims across the Arctic sea as sheets of ice float by and points its swirly-twirly "horn" straight up into the sky.

What other animals live in the Arctic?

LET'S READ

If I Were Nocturnal

By Jennifer Cherry ★ Art by Monika Filipina

If I were nocturnal, I would wake up when the world grows dark and the moon comes out.

I would walk to the park and call to my friends, "Hello, Beaver! Hello, Skunk! Hello, Raccoon! Come out and play with me!"

LET'S READ

Beaver would teach me to build a dam of sticks and mud. Then Raccoon and Skunk would help me hunt insects and find berries for a midnight picnic in the grass.

After our snack, we would play hide-and-seek
in the shadows and watch spiders spin webs.
When the sun started to rise, I would say,
"Good night!" and walk home.

LET'S READ

Then, as the birds began to sing, I would put on my pajamas and get into my bed.

If I were nocturnal, I would sleep all day and then wake up with the rising moon.

Alphabet, Interrupted

By Sarah Meade ★ Art by Joëlle Dreidemy

LET'S READ

LET'S READ

Bedtime in the Barnyard

By S. Dianne Moritz ★ Art by Anna Jones

Hush, little calf, don't moo, moo, moo.
Back to the barn. Bedtime for you.

LET'S READ

Hush, little colt, don't *neigh, neigh, neigh.*
Come settle down in the clean, fresh hay.

Hush, little lamb, don't *baa, baa, baa.*
Snuggle in now with your mama.

LET'S READ

Hush, little kitten, don't *mew, mew, mew.*
Cuddle up close. Come here now, you.

Hush, little chick, don't peep, peep, peep.
Scoot to your coop and go to sleep.

Hush, Mr. Rooster, please don't crow.
Take a snooze in the soft moonglow.

Sweet dreams, barnyard. Good night, sleep tight.
We'll see you tomorrow in the morning light.

LET'S READ

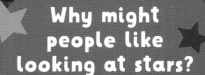

Why might people like looking at stars?

Here Come Stars

By Marguerite Chase McCue ★ Art by Kim Barnes

Fade away sun,
Fade away light.
Here comes evening,
Here comes night.
Day is done,
Day is through.
Here come stars
On midnight blue.

LET'S READ

LET'S EXPLORE

Let your little kid's excitement run wild as they explore nature. With these stories and activities, you can help your child learn more about the wonders of the world by encouraging them to experience the outdoors, observe wildlife, and question how things happen. Tap into their natural curiosity and set out on an adventure to see how your little explorer will grow and learn.

4 NATURE ACTIVITIES!

LEAF RUBBINGS

Collect fallen leaves outside. Place a leaf on a flat surface, and put blank paper over the leaf. Using the side of a crayon without a wrapper, rub over the leaf.

TRY rubbing a white crayon over paper on top of the leaf. Then run a marker over the top to reveal the leaf-print.

FRUIT FUN

Place slices of fruits, such as apples, oranges, and bananas, on a plate. Have your child close their eyes and guess what each fruit is based on touch, smell, and taste.

SHADOW ART

Set a stuffed animal or action figure in a sunny spot on pavement. Trace the object's shadow with chalk. Go back to the same spot at a different time of day and trace the shadow again.

How are the shadows different?

COUNT ON NATURE

Head outdoors and look for things you can count. Can you count groups of things you see up to 10?

| 1 | 2 | 3 | 4 |
| FLOWER | INSECTS | BIRDS | ROCKS |

What else do you see?

LET'S EXPLORE

Nature Pattern

Nature loves to do the same thing over and over again. Look at a tree. Branches grow more branches. Mathematicians call this a **fractal** (FRACK-tuhl).

Look at the repeated pattern!

There is a pattern in the snowflake.

This shell repeats in a swirl.

Look closely at a snowflake, a fern, or a pine cone. You'll see the same shape repeated in smaller and smaller sizes. **Where else can you see fractals?** Go on a nature walk to look for more!

Make Pretend
BINOCULARS

≥You Need≤

- ★ 2 cardboard tubes
- ★ Stickers
- ★ Markers
- ★ Tape
- ★ Hole punch
- ★ Yarn

Craft a pair of pretend binoculars to take on your ≥nature walk.≤

1 Decorate.

Decorate the cardboard tubes with stickers, markers, and other supplies.

2 Tape.

Tape the tubes together.

3 Punch.

Punch a hole in each tube.

4 Thread.

Thread a piece of yarn through each hole and tie a knot.

Animal HOMES

Check out homes built by wild critters!

Prairie dogs dig homes deep in the ground. These homes, called *burrows*, have many small spaces for eating and sleeping. The spaces are connected by tunnels.

Ruff! We bark!

Buzzzzzz

Some honeybees live in tree hollows. Their bodies create wax. The bees chew on the wax until it's soft. They use the wax to build a nest.

I love my lodge!

The entrance to a lodge is under water. A beaver must swim to get inside!

A **beaver** makes a home called a *lodge*. Beavers build lodges in streams and creeks. To make a lodge, beavers stack logs, sticks, and rocks. Beavers add mud to hold everything in place.

Weaver ants live in trees. They make nests out of tree leaves. First, weaver ants work as a team to gather leaves. Then they bind the leaves with a sticky silk.

Masterpiece!

What other animal homes can you see? Go outside, and try to spot bird nests, anthills, and more. (Don't touch the homes, just look at them!)

Reading Clouds!

Clouds come in different shapes and sizes.

Feathery clouds are often a sign of fair weather.

Dark clouds usually mean a storm is on the way.

White, puffy clouds are usually a sign of fair weather. But if they start to get dark, watch for rain.

Look up at the sky. Are there clouds? What do they look like?

LET'S EXPLORE

Track the MOON

When night falls, the moon appears in the sky! Let's find out more about the moon.

Watch the moon from the same spot each night for a week. Draw what it looks like. What do you notice?

The surface of the moon is very dusty.

The moon circles Earth. It takes about a month to make one full trip.

Sunlight hits the moon at different angles during the month. This makes it look like the moon changes shape. But it doesn't!

Where Does FRUIT Grow?

A banana plant can be taller than a giraffe.

Bananas grow upside down in bunches.

Kiwis grow on high vines.

Watermelons grow on vines on the ground.

Strawberries grow on plants on the ground.

Grapes grow on vines that climb up high.

Some types of grapes can be dried into raisins.

1-2-3 FRUIT SALAD

Use fruit to make a colorful, juicy snack!

You Need

- ★ 1 teaspoon honey
- ★ 2 teaspoons raisins (or chopped nuts)
- ★ 3 tablespoons plain yogurt
- ★ 4 grapes
- ★ 5 banana slices
- ★ 6 cantaloupe chunks
- ★ 7 kiwi slices
- ★ 8 strawberry slices
- ★ 9 blueberries

Tip:
If you're going to store the salad for later, consider coating the fruit in a bit of citrus or pineapple juice to help preserve it.

1 Prep.

Grown-up: Chop the nuts and cut the fruit.

2 Combine.

Combine the ingredients in a bowl.

3 Stir.

Stir 10 times.

How Do Vegetables Grow?

What is your favorite veggie?

Carrots are roots.

Carrots grow under the ground.

Potatoes are tubers.

Potatoes grow under the ground.

These are flowers.

Broccoli grows above the ground.

These are leaves.

Lettuce grows above the ground.

The peas grow inside an outer pod.

Each little piece of corn is called a kernel.

Sugar snap peas grow on vines above the ground.

Corn grows on stalks above the ground.

Tomatoes are fruits that are nutritionally considered vegetables.

Tomatoes grow on vines above the ground.

What delicious foods!

Meet the Dinosaurs!

T. rex

What does its name mean?
T. rex's full name is Tyrannosaurus rex (tie-RAN-uh-SAW-rus reks). This means "king of the tyrant lizards."

Why did T. rex have such tiny arms?
Scientists don't know for sure. But some think their small size made it harder for other dinosaurs to bite them!

What size was T. rex?
T. rex could weigh about the same as five small cars. And it could grow as long as a school bus!

Does it have living relatives?
Birds are descended from dinosaurs like T. rex.

LET'S EXPLORE

Apatosaurus

Were Apatosaurus babies big?
Babies hatched from eggs that were smaller than soccer balls.

How long was its neck?
It was longer than three giraffe necks!

How did it use its tail?
Some scientists think it snapped its tail to make a loud noise and scare off other dinosaurs.

Triceratops

How did it use its frill?
It may have used the frill, or bony plate, on its head to show off to other dinosaurs.

Why did it have horns?
Triceratops may have used its horns to defend itself from enemies.

What was for dinner?
It ate plants. With hundreds of teeth, it could easily gobble up yummy greens.

Cool Habitats

A habitat is a place where living things can get what they need. Check out these two habitats!

Tide pools are small pockets on a rocky shore where water is left behind when the tide goes out.

Who lives here? Animals such as crabs, starfish, and sea anemones can be found in tide pools.

 **+**  **+**

At high tide, the ocean water level rises, filling in and covering the tide pools.

The best time to visit a tide pool is at low tide.

This is a tide pool.

LET'S EXPLORE

The saguaro cactus grows in the hot, dry deserts of Arizona, California, and Mexico.

Some deserts are hot. Others are cold. Some are flat. Others have mountains or dunes.

What type of habitat is it where you live?

Deserts
Deserts are places that get very little rain.

Bearded Dragon

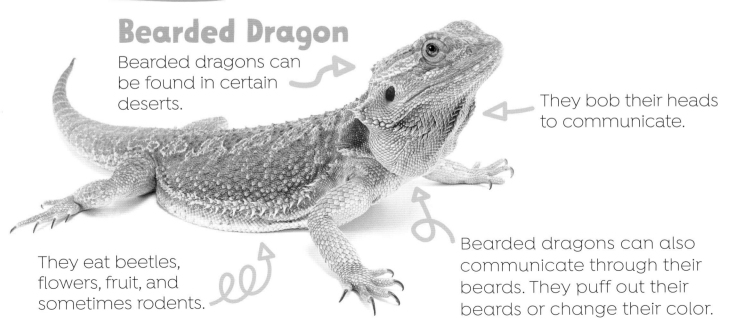

Bearded dragons can be found in certain deserts.

They bob their heads to communicate.

They eat beetles, flowers, fruit, and sometimes rodents.

Bearded dragons can also communicate through their beards. They puff out their beards or change their color.

Animal Families

Many wild animals live in families. Let's meet a few!

A group of dolphins is called a *pod.*

Dolphins swim in groups. Some groups have just moms and babies. The moms work together to care for the young. They protect the babies and help them find food.

Marmosets are a type of monkey. In marmoset families, dads do a lot to care for babies. They carry the babies around on their backs. They clean and play with the babies too.

A group of marmosets is called a *troop.*

LET'S EXPLORE

Some prides have up to 40 lions.

Lions live in groups called *prides*. Female lions run the pride. They hunt for food and raise the cubs. Male lions help guard the pride. While the parents work, the cubs play!

What other animal families can you think of?

A family of **wolves** is called a *pack*. Grown-up wolves live in a pack with their young. Packs travel and hunt together. Every member of the pack looks after new pups.

Baby wolves are called *pups*.

LET'S EXPLORE

SPOTTING SHADOWS

These shadows look like the penguins. That's because the penguins' bodies block the sun from shining on the ground.

Can you make silly shapes with your shadow?

If the sun is **behind** an object, like a penguin, the shadow will be in **front** of the object.

LET'S EXPLORE

If the sun is **in front of** an object, the shadow will be **behind** the object.

If an object's **side** is to the sun, the shadow will be **next to** the object.

If clouds **block** the sunlight, there won't be a shadow.

TRY IT OUT!

Find a sunny spot outside. Look at your shadow. Where do you think the sun is? In front of you, behind you, or to the side of you?

Recycled Bird Feeder

Bird Bonanza

Meet some birds and find out where in North America they live.

Black-capped chickadee

I live in the North.

I live in the East.

Tufted titmouse

Steller's jay

I live in the West.

Mourning dove

I live in all states, and I feed off the ground.

You Need

* Milk carton
* Duct tape
* Stickers
* Jumbo craft stick
* Twine
* Birdseed

Before You Begin

Adult: Cut out a large section from the front of the carton, leaving space at the bottom for birdseed.

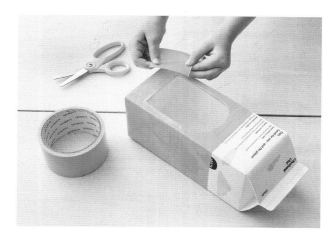

 **Cover.**

Cover the milk carton in duct tape.

 **Decorate.**

Decorate with stickers.

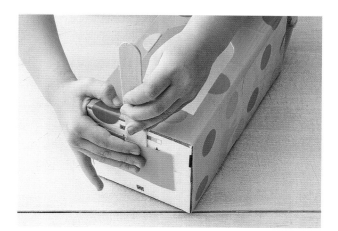

 **Tape.**

Tape the craft stick to the bottom of the carton.

 **Add.**

Add twine to the top of the carton with tape. Then hang the bird feeder outside.
Don't forget to add the birdseed!

LET'S DISCOVER

Little kids are learning new things about the world around them every day. Introduce your child to the world of STEAM (Science, Technology, Engineering, Arts, and Math) by fostering curiosity at home. Through fun experiments and activities, your child will question, explore, and play. Help your child find and chase their passions—even if they change from week to week!

MAKE A RAINBOW

Put a glass of water on a sheet of white paper. Shine a flashlight through the glass.

ASK: What do you see?

You can use fridge magnets or magnetic blocks for this activity!

GO MAGNET FISHING

Tie a piece of string to a magnet. Put a variety of items on the ground and go fishing for them!

ASK: Which items does the magnet pick up? Which items does the magnet not pick up?

THE SHAPE OF WATER

Pour water into a cup. Pour the water from that cup into another cup of a different size. Keep pouring the water from one cup into another.

ASK: How does the water move from cup to cup? What happens to the shape of the water each time you pour it?

BUILD A TOWER

Use cut-up apple pieces and toothpicks to build a tower. Measure the height of the tower.

ASK: How did you make it so tall? How could you make it taller and stronger?

LET'S DISCOVER

Why Do Boats Float?

1 Roll.

Roll a piece of modeling clay into a ball. Gently drop it into a bowl of water. What happens?

2 Make.

Use another piece of clay to make a boat with a large bottom and short sides.

3 Try.

Gently set the clay boat onto the water. What happens?

Ask:

How much weight can the boat carry? How many pennies can you add before it sinks?

LET'S DISCOVER

244

How Does Water Move?

You Need

* Water
* Wax paper
* Toothpick
* Paper towel
* Sandpaper

Ask: How are the wax paper, paper towel, and sandpaper different? Why do you think water acts differently on each?

1 Sprinkle.

Sprinkle a few drops of water on a piece of wax paper.

2 Move.

Use a toothpick to move the drops of water. What happens when the drops touch?

3 Move.

Try this again on a paper towel. Can you move the water? What happens to the paper towel?

4 Move.

If you have some sandpaper, try again. Can you move the water? Can you pour the water off the sandpaper?

LET'S DISCOVER

SCIENCE meets ART

MESS ALERT

You Need

* Baking soda
* Food coloring
* Distilled white vinegar

1 Place.

Place a muffin tin on a baking sheet. Add ¼ cup baking soda to each muffin cup.

2 Drop.

Put 10–15 drops of food coloring into each cup (one color per cup).

3 Pour.

Quickly pour the vinegar into each muffin cup until it fizzes.

Explain
As baking soda and vinegar mix, they change each other and make new things. One of those new things is a gas that makes the mixture foam up with lots of little bubbles.

LET'S DISCOVER

 **Paint.**

Paint the coffee filter with the colors from the science experiment. Let it dry.

 **Pinch.**

Pinch the coffee filter in the middle to create the flower's center.

 **Tape.**

Tape one end of the fuzzy stick to the pinched end of the filter.

4 Place.

Place your flowers in a vase or small cup.

TIP!
To create the flowers without doing the science activity, use watercolors to paint the coffee filters.

>You Need<

★ Colors from science experiment
★ Paintbrush
★ Basket coffee filters
★ Tape
★ Fuzzy sticks
★ Vase or small cup

Fresh Water, Salt Water

You Need

* 2 large, clear cups
* Towel
* Warm water
* Table salt
* Blue food coloring
* 2 of many different objects

Ask:

What happens to sinking objects when there is salt in the water?

LET'S DISCOVER

1 Place.

Place the cups on a towel. Pour 1½ cups of warm water into each cup.

2 Add.

Add ⅓ cup of salt to one cup to make salt water. Stir until the salt is mixed in.

3 Add.

Add a drop of blue food coloring to the fresh water to tell the glasses apart. Stir.

4 Place.

Place one of the same object in each cup. What happens?

Try experimenting with these objects

 2 balls of foil

 2 plastic toys

 2 crayons

 2 eggs

 2 metal spoons

 2 small tomatoes

Make a SPEEDY BOBSLED

In a race, some bobsleds can go as fast as a car on the highway.

Add weight to your bobsled and time it to see if it goes faster. What else would change the speed?

Once done with your bobsled and track, lean the top of the track against a chair or table. Then race your bobsled down the track.

LET'S DISCOVER

* Cardboard tube
* Scissors
* Paint

* Paintbrush
* Tape
* 2 plastic bendy straws

* 3-foot-long piece of cardboard

MESS ALERT

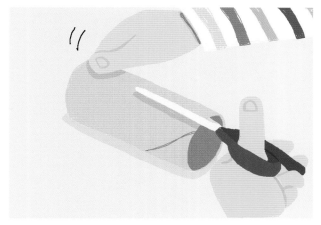

1 Cut.

Cut the cardboard tube open.

2 Paint.

Paint the cardboard tube.

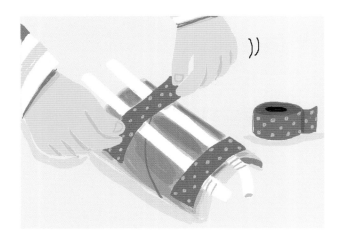

3 Tape.

Tape the straws to the bottom of the bobsled. Have the short part of each straw bend, as shown.

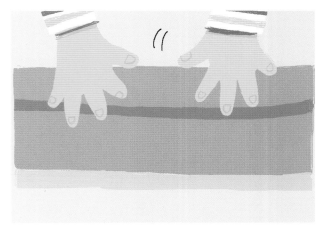

4 Fold.

To make the track, fold the sides of the cardboard up, leaving at least a 3-inch-wide base. Paint the bobsled track. Let it dry.

Pushing Is a Force

★ 9-inch-by-13-inch pan with water, ½ to ¾ full
★ Ping-Pong ball
★ Turkey baster

FORCE is a push or a pull when two objects interact.

1 Breathe.

Can you move the ball across the pan without touching the pan or the ball?

LET'S DISCOVER

2 Water.

Fill a turkey baster with water. Squeeze the water out to push the ball.

Breath or **Water**

Which push—your BREATH or the WATER—has more force? How can you tell?

LET'S DISCOVER

Can You Make It TALL?

Trees are tall. Skyscrapers are really tall! Strong materials—such as concrete, steel, brick, and wood help buildings stand tall. In a skyscraper, there are many floors and walls. Now it's your turn to be an engineer.

How will you build your tall tower?

1 Choose.

Choose a floor material as the base for your tower.

2 Connect.

Use connectors to add walls to the base.

3 Add.

Add floors, walls, and connectors to keep building up.

4 Decorate.

Place decorations.

How could you make your structure stronger?

Will these cups fall?

The straws help make it taller!

How many levels do you see?

Paper plate floors!

Can You Make It FLOAT?

Bases
* Containers
* Lids
* Craft sticks
* Craft foam

Adhesives
* Tape
* Clay
* Glue

Add-Ons
* Paper straws
* Paper
* Washi tape
* Aluminum foil

256

LET'S DISCOVER

Rowboats float. Kayaks float. Ships float too. Lightweight materials, such as wood and plastic, help boats to float. Many boats have a base, sides, and sails. Now it's your turn to be an engineer.

What kind of **floating boat** will you build?

1 Choose.

Choose a base for your boat.

2 Create.

Create and add details to your base.

3 Attach.

Use adhesives to attach sides, a sail, or other add-ons.

4 Test.

Test your boat on the water! Does it float?

Invent
What did you make?

Ahoy there!

Foam rafts with tape

Sail made with paper and tape

Lid from a peanut butter jar

Can You Make It MOVE?

You Need

Bases
* Boxes
* Foil
* Tubes

Axles
* Paper straws
* Pencils
* Markers

Wheels
* Lids
* Cups
* Clay

LET'S DISCOVER

Cars move. Trucks move. Trains move too. These vehicles have wheels and axles. The wheels and axles spin, which makes the vehicles go. A car has four wheels and two axles that connect to a base. Now it's your turn to be an engineer.

How will you build your moving vehicle?

Choose a base for your vehicle.

Make holes and push axles through the base.

Tape or glue wheels to the end of each axle.

Add decorations.

Invent What did you make?

Ready to roll!

Tube used for base

Water-bottle lids used for wheels

Hide and Seek

Some animals have colors and shapes that help them hide.

Colors and shapes that help animals blend in are called **CAMOUFLAGE.**

Can you find the **seahorse**?

Can you find the **katydid**?

LET'S DISCOVER

Can you find the **snake**?

Can you find the **arctic fox**?

Can you find the **frog**?

Can you find the **octopus**?

Can you find the **goat**?

Seed Balls

Make and plant colorful seed balls.

Let them dry, and give them as gifts!

 **Tear.**

Tear scraps of construction paper into tiny pieces. Place them in heat-safe bowls.

 **Boil.**

Grown-up: Boil water. Pour it over the paper pieces, covering them completely. Let the bowls sit for 2–3 minutes.

LET'S DISCOVER

>You Need<

* ★ Paper scraps
* ★ Heat-safe bowls
* ★ Spoon, blender, or food processor
* ★ Sieve or paper towel
* ★ Flower seeds

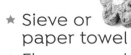

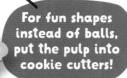

For fun shapes instead of balls, put the pulp into cookie cutters!

3 Mash.

Mash the mixture with a spoon, or pour it into a blender or food processor. Mix for 15 seconds. Repeat until it is a thick paste.

4 Drain.

Using a sieve or a paper towel, drain or squeeze the excess water from the paper pulp.

5 Add.

Add flower seeds to the pulp. (If the seeds need to be spaced out when planting, use only one seed per ball.)

6 Roll.

Form the pulp into balls (about golf-ball size). Plant them in soil in a pot. Water them, and watch the flowers grow!

LET'S SHARE KINDNESS

. . . .

Just like practicing letters, numbers, and colors, little kids need to work on making kindness a habit. These activities encourage little kids to show kindness to others, to be kind to themselves, and to work through their emotions. By being kind, kids are developing compassion and empathy toward others, traits that will serve them well in their future.

SIDEWALK MESSAGES

Brighten someone's day by drawing cheerful images and positive sayings on a sidewalk or driveway with chalk.

Try these sayings:
★ You are AWESOME!
★ Today is a GREAT day!

MAKE A GRATITUDE JAR

Each day, draw a picture of something you're grateful for. Put it in the jar. When the jar is full, empty it and look at all the things you are grateful for!

Being grateful means seeing the good things in your life. It's one way to be kind to yourself.

EMOTION CHARADES

Fill a bowl or hat with pictures of faces showing different emotions. Take turns picking a piece of paper from the bowl. One player acts out the emotion shown, using their face and body, but no words. Other players guess what the emotion is.

COMPLIMENTARY PICTURES

Encourage your child to draw a picture of a friend, family, or community member. Then ask your child to describe what they like about that person. Write their kind words on the drawing, then give it to that person.

LET'S SHARE KINDNESS

Pass It On

A Story About Spreading Kindness

By Sara Matson ★ Art by John Joven

Mouse was on her way to a picnic when she saw Frog stuck in a fishing net. Mouse chewed at the net until Frog was free.

"How can I thank you, Mouse?" Frog asked.

"No need," Mouse said. "Just pass it on."

Frog was hopping through the woods the next day when he heard a sneeze. Skunk was sick! Frog made her tea and read her a book.

LET'S SHARE KINDNESS

"How can I thank you, Frog?" Skunk asked.

"No need," Frog said. "Just pass it on."

Skunk was sniffing flowers the next day when she saw Bear get stung by a bee. Skunk put a cool cloth on his paw and filled up his honey jar.

"How can I thank you, Skunk?" Bear asked.

"No need," Skunk said. "Just pass it on."

Bear was on a walk the next day when he heard Mouse singing a sad song. She felt lonely. Bear asked if Mouse would come on a picnic with him.

"How can I thank you, Bear?" Mouse asked.

"No need," Bear said. "Just pass it on."

And, of course, she did.

How was kindness "passed on" in this story? How can you pass on kindness?

LET'S SHARE KINDNESS

My Moods

What are some of your moods?

Be Kind to Yourself

Say something else kind to yourself!

Look in the mirror. Say,

"I am a great kid—funny and smart, caring and kind. Yay, me!"

Here are other ways to be kind to yourself.

Be kind to yourself when something breaks or spills. **Ask for help to clean it up.**

Be kind to yourself when you make a mistake. **Keep trying!**

Be kind to yourself when you are angry. **Take five deep breaths to calm down.**

I'm Friendly

I wave and say hi to a new friend. I introduce myself and ask what her name is. Then I ask if she would like to play with me.

How can you be friendly today?

LET'S SHARE KINDNESS

New Friend

How do you feel when you say hello to someone new?

Someone new moved in next door.
I think she's my age—just turned four.

She's at her window looking down.
Is that a smile or a frown?

Mom says that I will never know
unless I go and say hello.

Sometimes it's scary to say hi,
but maybe I had better try.

Just then she opens her front door.
I open mine—a crack, then more.

And though we're both a bit afraid,
we say hello. A friend is made!

TRACE and BREATHE

Finger tracing is a quiet activity that can help you relax. Sit in a quiet spot. Trace each pattern with a finger. Breathe in and out slowly as you trace.

LET'S SHARE KINDNESS

TOSS and TALK

Play this game with an adult. Take turns tossing a coin onto the page. Say the emotion the coin lands on. Tell about a time when you felt that feeling. Then mark the board. Try to get 4 boxes in a row (across, down, or diagonally).

LET'S SHARE KINDNESS

Playing at the Park

By Christy Thomas ★ Art by Violet Lemay

Luna loves to play in the sandbox with Hazel.

One day, Luna sees Hazel playing with Jaxon.

Luna wants to play. But what if Hazel only wants to play with Jaxon and not with Luna?

How do you think Luna feels? Why?

LET'S SHARE KINDNESS

Hazel sees Luna by herself. "Want to play with us?" Hazel asks.

"Yes!" says Luna.

Luna, Hazel, and Jaxon play in the sandbox for the rest of the afternoon.

How do you think Luna feels now? Why?

Hello, World!

When you learn a new language, you can connect with people and show you care about them. Try saying hello in these languages!

Bonjour
French
(Bohn-JURR)

Hello
English
(heh-LOH)

Konnichiwa
Japanese
(koh-NEE-chee-wa)

Hola
Spanish
(OH-lah)

Jambo
Swahili
(JAHM-boh)

Nǐ hǎo
Mandarin Chinese
(NEE how)

Namaste
Hindi
(NUH-muh-stay)

LET'S SHARE KINDNESS

Protect-the-Planet BINGO

There are many small ways to help protect Earth. Can you do 3 things from the bingo card below?

Use a reusable water bottle. 	Turn off lights when you leave a room. 	Make a toy or game out of recycled items. 
Walk or ride somewhere you'd normally drive. 	Learn something new about the planet. 	Collect rainwater to water a plant.
Turn off the water when brushing your teeth. 	Find 3 items to recycle. 	Only take what you'll eat. 

Mail a Hug

You Need

- ★ Marker
- ★ Paper
- ★ Scissors
- ★ Glue stick
- ★ Envelope

Make this sloth and send it to someone you would like to hug!

Draw a sloth. Also draw 2 big circles, 2 small circles with eyes, and 1 heart.

Cut out the sloth, circles, and heart.

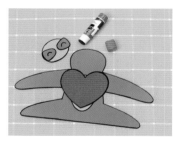

Glue a big circle and the heart onto the body. Glue the smaller circles onto the face and then glue the face to the body.

If you'd like, add a drawing or message to the heart. Then fold the sloth's arms and legs in. Put it in an envelope.

LET'S SHARE KINDNESS

CARDS That SPARKLE

Sending someone a care card is an act of kindness.
Follow the directions below to make cards that sparkle!

You Need

- ★ Water
- ★ Watercolor paper
- ★ Watercolor brush
- ★ Watercolor paints
- ★ Salt

Before You Begin
Adult: Cut 9-by-12-inch pieces of watercolor paper in half.

MESS ALERT

1 Paint.

Paint a light layer of water over a piece of watercolor paper. Use watercolor paints to make a design.

2 Sprinkle.

While the paint is still wet, sprinkle it with salt. The salt will make small white spots, like stars or snowflakes.

3 Brush.

Allow the paint to dry completely, then brush off any remaining salt.

4 Fold.

Fold the paper in half to make note cards.

Thank you!
I love you!
You are special!

5 Write.

Write a note in each card.

Ask an adult to help you send the cards to friends, family members, or teachers.

Game Time

By Christy Thomas ★ Art by Melanie Grandgirard

Jeffrey and Max are playing a new board game.

It's Jeffrey's turn. "Yes!"
he cheers. "I win! I win! I win!"

"You always go first and win," Max says. "I don't want to play anymore."

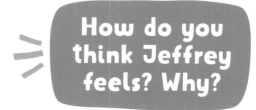

How do you think Jeffrey feels? Why?

LET'S SHARE KINDNESS

"We could play a different game," Jeffrey says. "And this time, you can go first."

"OK. I'll play," says Max. Max and Jeffrey take turns.

"Good job, Max!" Jeffrey says.
"That was fun!" says Max. "What should we play next?"

How do you think Jeffrey feels now? Why?

Random Acts of KINDNESS

Even the simplest act of kindness can make a big difference. Try out these ideas to spread kindness at home, with your friends, and in the community.

AT HOME

★ Draw hearts or smiles on sticky notes for someone.
★ Say I love you!
★ Help with a chore that someone usually does alone.
★ Ask someone about their day.

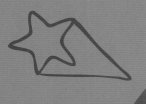

WITH YOUR FRIENDS

★ Help someone if they fall on the playground.
★ Tell a friend something you like about them.
★ Let someone go ahead of you in line.
★ Tell a friend a joke.
★ Invite a new person to play.

IN THE COMMUNITY

★ Smile and wave when you pass someone.
★ Decorate rocks with nontoxic paints or markers. Leave them around your neighborhood.
★ Leave a thank-you note for your mail carrier.
★ Go on a gratitude walk. Talk about what you're grateful for.

LET'S SHARE KINDNESS

A Kinder Me

To be kinder to my family.
To be kinder to the cat.
To be kinder to the neighbors
when they stop me just to chat.
To be kinder to my best friends
and to kids I don't know well.
To be kinder to librarians
and my doctor, Dr. Bell.
To be kinder to the bus driver.
To the cheery restaurant crew.
To be kinder to myself
because I'm important, too!

Who is someone you want to be kinder to?

Talk About It

Use these questions to learn more about yourself and others.
Answer one question at a time.

If you could **FLY**, where would you go?

Is it harder for you to **GET MOVING** or to **STAY STILL**?

Who are your **HEROES**? Why?

Would you rather **MAKE** a present for someone or **BUY** one?

Who is best at making you **LAUGH**?

What was something **NOT SO GOOD** that happened today?

What was something **GOOD** that happened today?

LET'S SHARE KINDNESS

What would you do if you saw a friend **CRYING**?

What are **3** things you like about yourself?

Can you be **FRIENDS** with yourself?

What would you do if a friend asked to play with your **FAVORITE TOY**?

What are your favorite **SMELLS**?

What **SUPERPOWER** do you wish you had?

What is **1 HELPFUL** thing you did today?

How do you like to **RELAX**?

LET'S SHARE KINDNESS

What Does Your Little Love?

Pick your child's favorite thing and do these activities together!

SUPERHEROES

CREATE Superhero Costumes (48–49)
MOVE Hero Moves (126–127)
PUZZLE Super Friends (190–191)

RAINBOWS

PRETEND Stick Wands (44–45)
COOK Rainbow Pizza (72–73)
SING The Rainbow Slide (106–107)
SHARE KINDNESS Trace and Breathe (272)

DINOSAURS

PRETEND Excavation Station (43)
CREATE Plate-o-saurus (100–101)
SING Dino Breakfast (108–110)
PUZZLE Dino Match (175)
EXPLORE Meet the Dinosaurs! (232–233)

SPACE

PRETEND Jetpack Adventure (34–35)
CREATE Super Spaceship (80–81)
SING Rocket Trip Surprise (111)
PUZZLE On the Moon (178–179)
EXPLORE Track the Moon (227)

Tell us what your kid loves with #myhighlightskid.

UNICORNS

PRETEND Magic Puppet Pals **(52–53)**
PUZZLE Unicorn Match **(181)**
READ Ocean Unicorn **(207)**

CONSTRUCTION

PRETEND Construction Zone Fun **(42)**
LAUGH Construction Zone **(166–167)**
SHARE KINDNESS Playing at the Park **(274–275)**

STUFFED ANIMALS

PLAY Stuffie Jump **(11)**
PRETEND Stuffie Checkup **(38–39)**
SING Bandages **(121)**
MOVE Stuffie Dance **(134–135)**

FLOWERS

PLAY Flower Power **(19)**
CREATE Fancy Flowers **(86–87)**
LAUGH Community Garden **(158–159)**
PUZZLE In the Garden **(176–177)**
DISCOVER Science Meets Art **(246–247)**

MONSTERS

COOK Squiggle Cookies **(68–69)**
CREATE Monster Pals **(88–89)**
SING The Glumps **(113)**

ROBOTS

CREATE Recycled Robot **(84–85)**
SING Made of Shapes **(112)**
DISCOVER Can You Make It Move? **(258–259)**

... crafts and science experiments to create!

Discover
High Five

The monthly magazine for 3-6 year olds! Inside you'll find ...

... yummy food to make!

... Hidden Pictures to find!

Highlights
HIGHLIGHTS.COM
High Five
Join In!

Find this hidden pizza!

Your kid could be here! Send us your photos at Highlights.com/ HighFive.

To subscribe, scan this code or visit highlights.com/ InspireFun.

HONEY

... dinos and other awesome creatures to learn about.

... stories and poems to read!

I love you!